EAT MY
SCHWARTZ

EAT MY SCHWARTZ

Our Story of NFL Football, Food, Family, and Faith

GEOFF AND MITCH SCHWARTZ

WITH SETH KAUFMAN

ST. MARTIN'S PRESS ☙ NEW YORK

www.stmartins.com

Dedication page photo courtesy of Fred and Brenda Schwartz

Design by Jonathan Bennett

The Library of Congress Cataloging-in-Publication Data is available upon request.

ISBN 978-1-250-08921-2 (hardcover)
ISBN 978-1-250-08922-9 (e-book)

Our books may be purchased in bulk for promotional, educational, or business use. Please contact your local bookseller or the Macmillan Corporate and Premium Sales Department at 1-800-221-7945, extension 5442, or by e-mail at MacmillanSpecialMarkets@macmillan.com

First Edition: September 2016

10 9 8 7 6 5 4 3 2 1

We dedicate this book to our grandfather, Norman Schwartz, our biggest fan! As much as you were so proud of us . . . we we're so proud of you!

Also to the fans that love football, faith, family, and food as much as we do . . . thank you for everything!

To everyone else . . . EAT OUR SCHWARTZ!

CONTENTS

ACKNOWLEDGMENTS   IX

INTRODUCTION   xiii

WARM-UP

1. FRIDAY NIGHT LIGHTS: IT ALL STARTS WITH A MEAL   3

FIRST DOWN

2. HIGH SCHOOL CONFIDENTIAL   11

3. THE QUARTERBACK SNEAK   31

4. DOUBLE MAJORS   43

SECOND DOWN

5. THE CHOSEN ONES: GETTING DRAFTED   71

6. LEARNING THE ROPES   93

7. ROOKIES AND RELIGION   119

THIRD DOWN

8. MY BROTHER'S KEEPER   133

9. RAISING ARIZONA AND MASTERING THE BODY   149

10. THE BRUNCH OF INFAMY   171

TOUCHDOWN

11. GETTING SEASONED   183

12. THE STREAK: STAYING IN SHAPE

AND DECOMPRESSING   197

13. GETTING BETTER (SORT OF) ALL THE TIME   205

14. POSTGAME HIGHLIGHTS   217

EXTRA POINTS

15. TWO-MINUTE DRILLS—QUICK TAKES

ON LIFE IN THE NFL   225

16. DINNER WITH THE SCHWARTZES   249

POSTGAME DINING

ACKNOWLEDGMENTS

Geoff

This book was a team effort. Actually, it was a multiple team effort.

Eat My Schwartz would never have happened without the vision and moxie of Courtney Parker, Deryk Gilmore, and Markus Hoffman. Thank you for realizing Mitch and I have a story to tell, helping us shape it and connecting us to the right people to make it happen.

Those people include Seth Kaufman, who was invaluable in

capturing our voices and sensibilities, and fine-tuning the book; our editor Marc Resnick, who took a chance on us and made this process an amazing one.; and all the great team at St. Martin's Press.

I'd also like to thank our wonderful television team at T-Group, who came up with our brilliant title—Jennyy Daly, Rob Lobl, our show creators, Courtney Parker (again) and Charles Cook—first publishing, next television, and then the WORLD!

We'd also like to thank the NFL and the teams that made our dreams of playing football a reality.

Our journeys have been shaped by so many wonderful and giving people. We'd like to thank our friends, teachers, coaches, teammates, and fans who have touched our lives in so many different ways.

For obvious reasons, this book could never have happened without our parents. Less obvious is how much they worked on the book, sharing memories, fleshing out the details and chronology. Their unwavering love and their support has been a true gift.

And speaking of gifts, I need to thank Alex for being my greatest inspiration and for taking naps so I could collaborate on the book. And, of course, Meridith for being my guiding light, my biggest fan and for always pushing me to be my best. I couldn't have gotten this far without you.

Mitch

What Geoff says. And endless thanks to my greatest inspiration, my new fiance and soon-to-be wife, Brooke!

INTRODUCTION

We are big.

We are so big that when I was a teenager, I got sick of people asking me about my size. I actually thought about having a T-shirt made. The front would say:

6'6"

340 lbs

Size 18

And the back of the shirt would say:

Now you know!

Twelve years later, I still think about wearing this shirt sometimes, because when I go out in public—at restaurants, in airports, at the supermarket, pretty much everywhere—people still ask me the same three questions: How tall are you? How much do you weigh? What size shoes do you wear? I don't mind the questions anymore, though. I'm a lot less self-conscious than my teenaged self.

My "little" brother Mitch—he's 6'5", 320 pounds, with size 18 shoes—doesn't mind the questions either.

As professional athletes we know size does matter. Mitch and I are offensive linemen. We push people, block people, and punch people for a living. It is challenging, physical work to compete against some of the best-conditioned athletes in the world.

Our size has had an impact on our lives in many ways—it has helped us earn scholarships. It has forced us to learn about food and nutrition and live healthier lives. It has helped us earn more money than we ever dreamed of earning. It has opened doors to new projects and people we never thought we'd meet. It has helped us spend thousands of hours practicing and playing a game we love.

But it takes a lot more than size to be successful in the National Football League.

This is the story of our journeys through the world of football, and about the hard work, perseverance, faith, and support that helped us succeed.

But we couldn't have gotten where we are without having a nurturing family that valued sports and fellowship as a way of celebrating life, and that valued putting effort into whatever we were doing: going to school, playing sports, cooking a meal.

Actually, make that many meals.

For all our girth, the fact remains that there have been bigger, faster, quicker, stronger, more experienced guys than Mitch and me at every level—high school, college, and the NFL—which means we had to develop other skills and strengths to combine with our size.

You can't teach size, the saying goes. But there are plenty of other things to learn about the game and about ourselves. And we are still learning.

WARM-UP

1

FRIDAY NIGHT LIGHTS: IT ALL STARTS WITH A MEAL

It's Friday evening, December 19, 2003, the first night of Hanukah. At our house in West L.A.—the place my brother Mitch and I have called home our entire lives—that means a few things. For one, our uncle Fred and his family will be there and so will our friends the Weinsteins. Every year we go to the Weinsteins' house for a Passover seder and every year they come here to celebrate Hanukah, the Jewish holiday known as the Festival of Lights.

It also means Mitch and I are in the kitchen, doing what we've always done every year at this time since we were old enough to help: making our grandmother's recipe for potato latkes. Latkes are potato pancakes, a traditional dish for the holiday. And for us, two rather large high school kids who love to cook and eat, making them is a major operation. First we do the grunt work: peeling fifteen pounds of potatoes and soaking 'em in big pots of water so they don't brown. Then we get the other ingredients ready: the bag of onions, salt, eggs, and olive oil.

No doubt plenty of cooks toss their latke spuds in a blender. But we are operating on old-school methods. We get the box grater out and we shred all those potatoes by hand, trying our best not to cut our fingertips off in the process. And that's harder than it sounds, because we've got gargantuan hands. I'm a 6'6" senior. My "little" brother, Mitch, a freshman, is about 6'4". And when we grate each potato down to that final tiny morsel, we have to slow down and carefully press that last bit of potato through the shredder or risk a bloodbath.

When we're done with the prep work, which also involves squeezing out the excess water from the grated potatoes and shredding all the onions, too—a big chunk of onion can overpower our Jewish flapjacks—we mix everything together, fire up a couple of frying pans, heat the oven to 200 degrees to keep the early batches warm, and go into mass production.

When the Weinsteins show up—Joel, who works with our mother at an L.A. law firm, Deborah, and their twin sons Perry and Adam, who are little kids I've known since they were babies—I start to think about all the meals we've shared together and I wonder about next year. I'm going away to college and I've been weighing scholarship offers from some major football programs, the kind of teams that play Bowl games at the end of December. Who knows if I'll be back here for Hanukah, or any of the other holidays we share together? I'm not a super-sentimental guy, but I am passionate about gathering around the table, bonding and breaking bread with family and friends to eat great food. It's the most basic communal human ritual there is.

Our dad, Lee, puts out the hors d'oeuvres and gets everyone drinks. In the kitchen, the sizzling continues as Mitch and I take turns manning four frying pans full of latkes, calibrating each one for that optimal fried golden-brown look that says they are done. It's funny: some people look at cooking as work or a chore, and some people might think of football as play, but for us, it's sort of the opposite. Mitch and I are not the most artistic guys on the planet—we don't paint or draw or play music—but cooking has become a creative outlet for both of us, something we enjoy exploring and experimenting with. We love the improvisational element of cooking, and the social element, too. Food, which is so important to us as athletes—it fuels our work—provides the forum for us to create meals that look good and taste fantastic. As fun as football is, as much as we love "playing," it definitely can be hard work.

By the time we join the others, my uncle Fred, aunt Brenda, and their twins, my super-cute three-year-old cousins Amanda and Heather, have arrived. Our conversations are wide ranging. L.A. is recovering from a big media circus around the indictment of Michael Jackson on charges that just make everyone shake their heads in disbelief and horror.

My uncle asks if we heard about Ben Roethlisberger, a junior at Miami of Ohio, ending his college career with a superb game against Louisville. "He threw four touchdowns in the first half and had a thirty-five to seven lead in the second quarter. Now he says he's going pro."

Joel and Deborah ask about the college recruitment process. Which colleges am I interested in? Which have I visited? What do I want to study? I have this idea that I'm interested in eventually being a lawyer, like my mom and Joel. So I'm thinking about studying history, which seems like a relevant field of study for a lawyer since there's a lot of reading and analyzing facts. I mention the names of a few schools that have offered me scholarships.

Joel asks my parents what they think.

"It's Geoffrey's decision," my dad says. "He's worked his tail off on the field and in school. And he's the one who is going to have to do the work."

My mom laughs. "I didn't believe Lee when he told me scholarships were a possibility. But it's happened. And now Lee and Geoff say it will happen for Mitchell, too."

"Geoff and Mitch have the size and athleticism," my dad says. "But I'm most proud of their work ethic and perseverance. They both had a big learning curve."

It's true. My brother's size and physique make him even more suited to the offensive line than I am. He's come on some of the college tours and we joke that we can practically see the recruiters making mental notes to send Mitch letters as soon as possible.

Adam and Perry ask when we are going to start the candle ceremony. For eight nights in a row, we light a candle called the "shamash" and then use that candle to ignite one candle for each night of the holiday. So on the first night we have two candles burning and on the eighth night we have nine. We do this to celebrate and give thanks for a miracle from the time around 174 B.C. when the Maccabees, Jewish warriors who faced seemingly insurmountable odds, defeated the massive forces of Antiochus, the murderous leader of Syria, and then retook the Temple in Jerusalem. There, they found a small jar containing only enough olive oil to light a menorah for a single day. But instead of going out, the oil burned for eight more days until new supplies arrived. It was a miracle, and a sign that God was looking out for the Jews.

As we light the candles we say a few prayers in Hebrew. Many families sing songs, like "Rock of Ages," but we Schwartzes don't have the greatest voices, so we opt to protect our guests' eardrums.

We head to the dinner table. My mom lights the Sabbath candles and we chant the blessing over the bread. And then it is time to eat. Mitch and I carry out the stacks of pancakes; the table is outfitted with bowls of sour cream, applesauce, and sugar—the condiments that we love to slather on each latke. Like the perfect hamburger, everyone has his or her own vision of what constitutes the perfect latke. Some believe fried onions and sour cream are the perfect combination. Others indulge in seemingly bizarre pairings of sour cream and applesauce. In that vein, Mitch is a proponent of sour cream with a little sprinkling of sugar, which he says is the perfect way to achieve maximum sensory overload: you get the salt, the potatoes, you get the oil and the fat, the sour cream gives you a little tartness, and the sugar gives you a little sweetness. Me? I'm a straight sour cream man.

"When was your first varsity high school game?" Joel asks.

I'm pretty sure he knows the answer. "Last year," I say.

He shakes his head in disbelief. "And they're offering you full scholarships?"

"A miracle," my uncle says. "But it's the season for miracles."

Everybody laughs.

FIRST DOWN

2

HIGH SCHOOL CONFIDENTIAL

Geoff

You've probably seen pictures of the high school Mitch and I attended. Set on eleven acres and located in a canyon between the Santa Monica Bay and the Santa Monica Mountains, Palisades Charter High School is sort of a fantasy American high school come to life. It's also not far from Hollywood. That proximity has made it the ideal setting for a ton of blockbuster movies, including *Freaky Friday*, *Old School*, and even the first Stephen King movie, *Carrie*. And if you haven't seen those movies, there's a good chance you've seen our school on TV. It's the high school setting for the kids in *Modern Family*.

In real life, the combination of a great L.A. location and the fact that it is a strong school academically means that it has attracted a who's who of Hollywood alumni in the fifty-odd years since it opened its doors. J. J. Abrams of *Lost* and *Star Trek* fame, will.i.am of the Black Eyed Peas, and that party goofball Redfoo of LMFAO—aka Stefan Gordy, the son of Motown Records founder Berry Gordy—are some of the more recent celebrities who went there. There were other pretty faces that attended besides mine: Christie Brinkley, an early supermodel, was a member of the class of '72.

Despite those big names, with nearly three thousand kids, most of whom are selected by lottery and bused from all over L.A., Pali, as all the kids call it, is hardly Beverly Hills High or the Harvard-Westlake School in terms of the city's privileged, big money institutions. To me, it was a great mix, with a real cross-section of kids you find in L.A. In that way, it was familiar to me. After preschool, my parents had always sent us to public schools where the student body was diverse: Chicano kids, African American kids, Asian kids, even Jews like me. Growing up where we did, in a wealthy part of L.A., a lot of neighborhood kids were sent to private schools, but I'm glad I went where I went. I think it helped reinforce some very basic life lessons, number one being: people are just people.

As far as sports at Pali High goes, NBA stars Steve Kerr and Kiki Vandeweghe played hoops for the Pali Dolphins.

But very few football players have cracked the NFL. To my knowledge, only QB Jay Schroeder, who played for the Redskins, Raiders, Bengals, and Cardinals, made it to the big time.

And that's interesting, because my first year there, when I was playing JV football, the school was a real football factory. Seven guys on the varsity team got Division 1 scholarships. By the time I made varsity the next year—go ahead, make a joke about me bringing down the team—the talent level had plummeted, no doubt because the coach who had helped Pali become a local powerhouse left the program.

But in ninth grade, I was totally thrilled to be in high school and have the chance to play three sports. Unlike a lot of my peers in the NFL—60 to 70 percent of pro players first started playing youth football between the ages of five to fifteen, according to the player's union—I didn't play on a Pop Warner team.

I was a football fan, of course—I grew up attending every UCLA home game with my parents—but in terms of offensive and defensive line skills, I arrived with zero experience.

There were two reasons for this. The main one, when I was twelve, was that football would have been too time consuming. That year, I had to study Hebrew and have weekly Bar Mitzvah lessons. The second reason was that even if I had managed to convince my parents that I could handle school, study Hebrew, and play baseball and basketball, I was over the weight limit for Pop Warner football.

Going out for high school football was a slightly sensitive

issue in my family. For one thing, my mom, who answers to both Olivia and Livie, worried that she'd be a bad Jewish mother if she let me play. Initially, she was concerned about Mitch and me getting injured. Although this is what she tells her friends now: "I started out worrying that they were going to get hurt—but then I realized it was the other players I should be worrying about. They were like trucks hitting small cars. Gradually I started to kind of feel like maybe this was their destiny."

For my dad, Lee, who grew up in Santa Rosa in Northern California and was a huge 49ers fan as a kid, the issue of high school football had been more painful. When it was time to start freshman year, his mother, like thousands of Jewish moms before and after her, had said, "No, Lee, you can't play football."

When my dad went to his first gym class, the gym teacher, who was also the football coach, walked over to where my dad was sitting and said in front of the entire class, "Hey, Schwartz, are you coming out for football this year?"

There was no way my dad was going to tell him the humiliating truth—that his mom wouldn't let him—so he said, "No. I'm going to concentrate on baseball and basketball."

"What a wimp," said the coach in front of the whole class.

We all laugh about that story now, especially since, ironically, the coach himself was Jewish, and was certainly in a position to understand that there is no higher authority than a Jewish mother.

today. Learning to read a totally alien language like Hebrew was cool, and it took discipline and focus. Plus I've always thought that discussing Bible stories is kind of like morality or philosophy classes for kids. You learn about right and wrong, about justice and injustice. I like how Judaism focuses on the positive. You do things not out of fear of something bad happening to you, but because you want to do good for its own sake.

But there's a joke that Hebrew school has wrecked more than a few careers of young Jewish athletes, and after becoming a Bar Mitzvah—the ancient Jewish ceremony when thirteen-year-old boys embrace adulthood—I stayed active in my synagogue for two years, attending Hebrew High. But while religion is a part of my family's life, it's not the be all and end all. When I got to high school and the work and sports commitments piled up, I asked my mom if I could just dial it back a little. She said if I got straight A's I could move on. There was only one thing to do: I got straight A's.

The other extracurricular activity that took up a lot of my time, besides sports, was a speech therapy class. I was a stutterer growing up. I didn't stumble on every word, but I had a noticeable stammer at times. My earliest memory of stuttering was being sent to speech therapy in elementary school. But I guess those sessions didn't work very well, so fortunately my parents found a wonderful private speech pathologist, Dr. Suzi Fosnot. I started seeing her privately twice a week for about ten years. It was great to have her support and guidance. Living with a mild disorder can be very hard on a kid. It certainly made me tougher—I was determined to say what I wanted to say. But it was not easy seeing the discomfort and even mockery on the faces of people as I struggled to communicate. I felt inadequate. There were kids who teased me and made jokes about my speech impediment. I got picked on for it. Even in my senior yearbook some people wrote thoughtless, insensitive messages. They'd write "S-s-s-so long" and stuff like that. They probably thought they were being funny, but that hurt. I guess these days that would be considered bullying. To me, it was just something I had to work through.

Having a stutter also taught me who my real friends were. I don't have that many close childhood friends that I've remained tight with. I had three buddies in elementary school, and we hung out after class, playing sports and video games. One of my pals Steve Nirenberg, who years later was a groomsman at my wedding, never mentioned my stutter, not even once. That was really important to me.

I owe so much to Dr. Fosnot, who I still keep in touch with. When I first met with her for an evaluation, she told my parents she wasn't sure if I would ever beat my stutter—that's how bad it was.

She encouraged me and taught me to slow down. She helped me get through my Bar Mitzvah speech. I don't know if you've ever seen the Oscar-winning movie *The King's Speech*, which is about England's King George VI and his battle to overcome a stutter and deliver a speech declaring war on Germany in 1939. But when I saw that movie, it hit me where I lived. I was terrified at the idea of speaking in front of a huge crowd for my Bar Mitzvah. What if I started stuttering? It would be a totally embarrassing, uncomfortable nightmare in front of everyone I cared about. Dr. Fosnot had me draw lines after every four words to get me to pause, which is exactly what they do in the movie when the King gives his big radio speech. Of course there were some differences: the King was alone with his speech therapist speaking to millions of his subjects; I was in a room packed with over a hundred people, reminding myself to breathe and pause. I nailed it and didn't stutter once.

I used to get stuck at the start of sentences sometimes, and there were certain letters, like *W*'s and *S*'s and *T*'s and *R*'s, and their specific sounds that gave me trouble. Words that start with *W* are really common—what, where, why, when—we use those a lot. If you start your voice a little bit before you pronounce the *W*, it helps gets the *W* sound out cleaner. I know that's a weird idea—starting your voice before you actually speak. But for me it meant relaxing, not feeling time pressure, and opening up my throat at the beginning of formulating a word.

Learning techniques like that was important to me. And then—not unlike football—improving my speech was all about practicing and working on sounds and phrases, over and over and remembering to slow down. As I got older, I also just got more comfortable in my own skin. Probably the last technique I developed that really helped me get over the stuttering was learning to temper my emotions. When I got really excited or really angry, the stutter would flare up. So as I learned to maintain a more even keel about life and events around me, my ability to speak clearly and smoothly really took off.

By the time I was a senior in high school, my stuttering had gone down to maybe a couple of times a day. And then, by the middle of my college career, it was almost completely gone. There are people that I met at college who didn't know I stuttered, and unless they read this now, they still don't.

My stuttering still surfaces on occasion, but only very rarely. If there's an upside to having a stutter, besides thickening my skin, it's that I'm probably more empathetic to disorders of all kinds; I know how "being different" with even the slightest abnormal condition can affect someone's life.

Being on the Palisades High football team was a great experience. I played center on the basketball team, so I'd had my fair share of banging under the rim. But playing the line—and I played both sides of the line my junior and senior years, and I served as the long snapper in punting situations—was a whole new level of physicality. Rarely in sports does brute force—speed, momentum, and muscle—combine with such focus, finesse, and teamwork. In baseball, there's the double play and the relay, but team coordination, when all the players are moving together, is rare. In basketball, there is a flow and spontaneity to the game. Sure, there are plays—pick and rolls, double screens, double teams, presses—but there is an improvisational quality to the game. Football has improvisational moments once a play develops, especially for QBs, running backs, and receivers. But each play begins with a carefully planned and orchestrated explosion of action and the imposition of one team's physical will over the other that, other than rugby and Australian rules football, you don't really get in any other team sport.

When I started working out, I made another big discovery. Because I'd been a good pitcher in Little League, I thought I was in okay shape. But looking back on it now, I just shake my head. The muscle and conditioning I needed for football was a whole other level from where I was at. I spent the entire year—and almost all of my sophomore year—on the JV squad. When I did get the call to join the varsity at the end of the year, it was to play on the defensive line, which is the safest place to put someone with no experience—they just told me to tackle anyone with the ball and knock over anyone who got in my way.

In my junior year we got a great new football coach, Jason Blatt. He was a no-nonsense guy and a straight shooter. He brought in Kelly Loftus as our offensive line coach. Kelly was a big influence on me and became a great friend of mine. He really pushed me hard starting my junior year. He and Coach Blatt came to me and said I had the potential to go far. I had the size and the athleticism that college football programs would be interested in. They shifted me to offensive tackle and started teaching me line skills and drills. That is when I really started to become a lineman.

It was incredibly strenuous—a whole other level from what I'd been doing previously. But I found I enjoyed that, too—hitting the dummies, hitting my teammates in drills, developing quickness at the line, and focusing on my footwork.

One of the teammates I met at Pali and who became a great friend and major influence on me was Duane "Duke" Manyweather, a six-foot, 300-pound half-Samoan dude. Duke and I anchored the line for Pali my junior year and, despite going our separate ways in college, we've always kept in touch and have anchored each other over the years. Duke is a true student of the game. He played for, and later coached at, Humboldt State. He has a degree in kinesiology, which is the study of the mechanics of body movements, and he has applied his knowledge to the science of football and conditioning. That education—and Duke's friendship— has been a blessing over the years. But back in high school, having Duke a year ahead of me was a real inspiration. He was the only guy on the team who went to the next level.

Probably my most important play in high school on the football field came in the final seconds of the last game of my junior year. We were driving down the field, trying to score the game-winning touchdown.

There was time for one more play and the opposing team intercepted.

I was so infuriated I took off after the cornerback, cutting across the field at an angle. I knew the game was over, but I did not want to give up a pick six on our last play of the game. I ran down the cornerback and tackled him on the 2-yard line. It was just one of those in-the-moment, super-competitive plays. And fortunately it was captured on videotape—just the kind of play any lineman would want for his highlight reel.

During that season, my father told my mother that, based on what he was hearing from coaches, he thought I had the talent and size to earn a football scholarship. My mom, who is a lawyer and not the kind of person who counts her chickens before they hatch (she is such a just-the-facts realist, it might be fair to say she won't even mention the eggs in the roost), refused to even think about it.

Right after my junior year, though, my mom had no choice. Big college programs started expressing serious interest, including some schools I was really into. Initially I had dreamed of going to UCLA. It was kind of in my blood, since my parents first met on campus and I went to pretty much every home game as a kid.

So it was natural that I wanted to go there. I think the recruiters knew I was a fan, and that might have worked against me. After getting invited to a Bruins training camp, they really didn't spend much effort recruiting me. Maybe they thought I was such a die-hard fan that they didn't have to spend any time with me or show some love. Or maybe they thought I wasn't a strong player. Or maybe someone on Karl Dorrell's UCLA recruiting staff just dropped the ball. Whatever the reason, as the process went on, I never felt like they were very interested.

At first I was upset that UCLA handled the process the way they did, but I started focusing on the other great programs wooing me. My two favorites were Arizona and Oregon, and there was *plenty* to love about both schools.

The offers increased after I went to some of the football camps run by Nike, Scout, and other organizations that summer. That was where college coaches and recruiters could actually see me work out and do my thing. The most intimidating camp was at USC. I stepped onto the field and we had a no-pads full scrimmage filled with big-time players from major high school programs around the country, guys with bodies and reputations far more imposing than mine.

The most fun and important camp for me was probably Stanford. Before that camp, I still thought baseball was the sport I would most likely pursue on a professional level. At Stanford, there was a split camp, with the first week focused on baseball and the second on football. That initial week was a real wake-up call for me. I got to compare my stuff with some of the best high school pitchers in California, and to pitch against some of the best hitters. The results were not great, and for the first time I realized I might not have what it takes to be a dominant pitcher at the next level.

If I couldn't take control at the collegiate level, well, the Major Leagues was not going to be an option.

While that was a shock—I'd played baseball ever since my dad started coaching my T-ball team when I was five years old, and had really excelled at the younger levels—the football camp was a blast. There was no dedicated offensive line focus, so instead I got to play tight end and spend the days blocking and catching passes. I loved it. Having so much fun was a much needed antidote after discovering I wasn't going to be the second coming of Cy Young.

In my senior year, as I weighed my future, I decided to quit the basketball team. It was a tough thing to do—I loved playing hoops and supporting my teammates. But I was looking at playing football for major Division 1 programs, and I was getting some ratings that made me want to focus on getting better. Tom Lemming, the premier high school football recruiting analyst, called me one of the five best line recruits in California. I went on to earn first team honors for All-City and Westside, and Rivals.com listed me among the top forty linemen in the country. All these honors—which, by the way, were not being handed to me for basketball—made me a little cautious. I didn't want to risk tearing up my legs on the hardwood, and I wanted to make sure I had the strength and skills to play college football, and to keep up my performance on the field, where I hadn't given up a sack in those last two years.

Actually, I was involved in two sacks, but they arose from

me playing on the other side of the ball as a defensive tackle. I loved playing both ways. When you are in high school and you feel so strong, you just want to play. Or at least I did. It feels great to be involved on almost every play, plus you feel a little like a throwback, like the hard-nosed Jim Thorpe, the gridiron great, who used to play both ways. I added to my sacks during my senior year with fifty-five tackles, including ten for a loss of yardage, three deflected passes, and one fumble recovery. Not that I'm counting or anything.

My decision to go to Oregon was quite easy. These days the Oregon Ducks are a perennial national powerhouse, but that wasn't quite the case when I arrived (although as the Ducks nation knows, 2000 and 2001 were pretty awesome seasons). But the choice for me was simple. Although I had great respect for Arizona coach Mike Stoops, Oregon felt like the place for me: a terrific college town with a great program and an offensive line coach, Neal Zoumboukos, I really connected with.

A veteran coach with three sons of his own, Coach Zoumboukos was a guy I felt I could learn from and relate to. Under head coach Mike Bellotti, Coach Zoumboukos had built up a family atmosphere that exuded success and togetherness. The program felt comfortable, like a place I wanted to be. I visited a bunch of other schools, but none of them gave off that same vibe. The night before my letter of intent was due, I talked with my parents about my options one final time. Once again, when I added everything up, Oregon felt like the right place. It was close enough to home, and played in the ultra-competitive Pac-10, which would put me up against some of the most talented players in collegiate football. It seemed like the right place to grow and prove myself.

The next day I woke up and faxed in my commitment letter. I didn't make a big deal about it, and neither did my parents. But a few months later, right before I went off to Oregon, my parents threw a surprise party at El Torito, a West Coast chain that has always been one of our go-to Mexican joints in the neighborhood. I've probably eaten about a hundred fajitas there, especially their "ignited" fajitas dish, where they pour tequila on a steak, chicken, and shrimp combo and flambé it at your table. To a hungry high schooler, this was a sizzling bit of heaven.

Mexican and South American food is a big part of our food culture in L.A. In fact, rice and beans may actually beat matzo ball soup as my first comfort food. That's because before we were old enough to go to preschool, my brother and I had a nanny named Vita from El Salvador, and we were insane for her cooking. To this day it is hard to think about rice without thinking of her delicious dishes packed with corn, beans, and onion.

My brother and I were on a first-name basis with the guys at a local joint called Fast Taco. We've gone there so often that the owner will come out and instruct his guys on preparing our burritos. For me, the burrito grande is light on my beloved rice and heavy on the chicken, cheese, and shrimp.

That evening at El Torito was perfect. Comfort food gets

its name for a reason. And when I think about it now, the menu that night—chicken and avocado rolls, flaming fajitas, street tacos—was filled with familiar delicious flavors that were perfect for celebrating with my friends, family, mentors, and teachers.

All my old coaches were there, not just from the football team, but Little League and basketball, too. There were old family friends, like my dad's pal Neil Berk, who once looked me dead in the eye at Burger King and told me I needed to cut out eating fries, literally taking the food right off my tray. And there was Kermit Cannon, who I met when I was thirteen on a travel baseball team. Kermit and I were still working together back then on my conditioning to make sure I was game-ready for Oregon. Seeing all the people who guided me and spent time working with me to be a better athlete and a better teammate, I felt beyond lucky. They had worked with hundreds, no, *thousands* of kids over the years. I had worked hard, but so had many of the people in the room. And now they were here to wish me well and see me off, into the unknown.

I loved being with them and thinking about where I'd been and where I was going. The whole thing was crazy: two years earlier, I had never played a down at offensive tackle. One year earlier, I was still thinking seriously about playing baseball. Now I was heading to a major Division 1 program on a full athletic scholarship to play football.

An athletic scholarship—or any scholarship, really—is

a major achievement. Anyone who earns one anywhere should be proud. But I didn't want it to end there. I was already thinking—wondering, dreaming—about the next step beyond college. And I wasn't even in school yet.

3

THE QUARTERBACK SNEAK

Mitch

When I arrived at Pali High in 2003, two years after Geoff got there, I was 6'4", weighed about 250 pounds, and had zero intention of playing football. Going into my freshman year I knew I wanted to pitch for the baseball team and that was it. You have to understand: I had had a pretty good run in Little League. My size and strength gave me an advantage when it came to throwing hard. We won our division and I was an All Star. It was great to experience success at a young age, and I was eager to see how I'd fare against the next level of competition.

Looking back, one of the other reasons I was so attached to baseball was that our dad was the coach of our Little League team and it was a really positive experience for all of us. Parents don't always have the time to interact with kids, but my dad made it a priority and he made it fun. My dad isn't a shouter. He wouldn't yell or belittle anyone. You know the guy who's even-keeled? The guy who, when he raises his voice, *that's* when you can tell when something's wrong? Well, that guy is our dad.

The rules about being part of a team—trying your hardest, doing your job, trusting and relying on others, picking up slack for your teammates if you are needed, cheering for you teammates—were basics for us. Our dad guided us in the lessons of teamwork and taught us to enjoy the effort that goes into accomplishing something, and then to enjoy the satisfaction of the accomplishment.

So while I liked football at the time—like Geoff, I had attended UCLA games with my parents, who graduated from the school in 1977, and I rooted for the 49ers on TV—I didn't spend a lot of time thinking about it the way I did baseball.

Fortunately, my dad, who had seen all the college scholarship interest that Geoff was getting, had other plans. He and Geoff floated the idea that, given my pitching "talents," I would be a natural quarterback.

I can hear you laughing. There are no 250-pound high school freshman quarterbacks anywhere in the known universe. But I was fourteen years old, so what did I know? As far as I was concerned, I was a pretty good athlete, and I loved the idea of throwing passes. I thought going out for JV quarterback was, if not a sure thing, then at least in the realm of possibility.

Those first two weeks at practice, I worked out as quarterback with the JV squad. I don't remember much of it, but evidently while my footwork and arm strength didn't blow the coaches away, my size sure did. One morning the coaches said they wanted to try me on the offensive line, which, I discovered later, had been my dad and Geoff's plan all along. I had never seen a blocking dummy, I couldn't tell you the difference between a two-point stance and a three-point stance. To me, a stunt was a trick you pulled—like telling an unsuspecting kid he should try out for quarterback—not a sneaky maneuver by defensive linemen who try to get past the offensive line by slanting or moving laterally at the snap instead of plowing straight ahead.

But at that point, I had been working out with the team— and the same tenets of sportsmanship and commitment that I learned in Little League surfaced immediately. I moved to the line without a single word of protest.

Let the record show, however, that I did get to play one series as QB in the first game of my freshman season. I took a snap from the shotgun position, stood in the pocket without moving an inch, and threw a 20-yard completion.

I think that means I have a very high passer rating.

I still love throwing footballs. Later, in college, I developed my own pregame routine. I'd head out on the field without my pads and toss the ball with my buddy Spencer Ladner, who played tight end. As we warmed up, we slowly moved farther and farther apart, increasing the distance of our throws until I got out to the 50-yard line. At this point the game wasn't catch anymore; it was more like target practice: hit the crossbar of the goalpost from 60 yards away.

I did it a number of times.

Obviously, being the younger brother of a sought-after football player in high school made me better known than the average incoming freshman. But high school is segmented—freshmen hang with freshmen, juniors with juniors, so my classmates weren't that aware of my brother. On sports teams, the social barriers break down a little bit; you meet kids from other grades. By the time I was a junior, though, Geoff was gone and I was my own person.

Who was that person? I was the quieter one then and I'm the quieter one now. I'm more low-key. I'm not a party guy. I don't drink much—socially or otherwise. I've sampled a variety of drinks in my day, but I just don't like the taste. While I'm very much a team player, I enjoy solitary pursuits: watching TV, gaming, reading, and cooking.

When I think of celebrating, I think of eating well. I'd rather go to a Brazilian *churrascaria* and sample the all-you-can-eat platters of meat that come around than go bar hopping. I love those places, not that I chomp away mindlessly like Homer Simpson come to life. Put it this way: when my parents and I celebrated my getting drafted, my mother said she felt sorry for the restaurant because I spent three hours savoring the never-ending parade of meats. Hey, I'm just committed to high-protein diets.

Of course, being a Jewish mother, she also enjoyed watching her son eat, I'm sure. What mother doesn't?

My football skills thrived at Pali High, and at the same time, my baseball career hit a plateau, as other kids caught up physically to me. My high school pitching career was solid but unspectacular. My once supersonic pitches that dominated in Little League weren't quite so intimidating against older competition. I was good but I needed to throw a lot harder to have a future in it. As for my own hitting career, it was pretty dull. The fact is, I didn't hit all that many homers for someone my size.

On the football field, hitting has a different meaning, and it was slowly dawning on me that I might have the chance to develop into a real football player. The first clue, obviously, was that I was usually bigger than everyone else on the field, so that was a plus. As a team, we were pretty bad, despite the best efforts of my teammates and our father-and-son coaches, Leo Castro and Aaronn Castro, and the assistant, Ron Evans. We only won nine games in my three years on varsity. We also lacked a dedicated offensive line coach—although Kelly Loftus, who also worked with Geoff, was very helpful in getting me ready for the football camps. But in terms of blocking skills and schemes, I wasn't getting a lot of hands-on guidance I'd need for the college game.

Despite all that, everyone kept saying that I was as good as or better than my brother. Even my brother said I was more of a natural than he was. That comparison was really important, and not because of any sibling rivalry. Knowing that Geoff got a lot of attention and went on to get a scholarship at a school with a major football program made me realize that I had the potential to be good. And I also realized it was up to me and nobody else to fulfill that potential.

I started cooking in high school as well. I owe this to my mom, the Food Network, a giant freezer in the garage, and being hungry all the time.

My mom was always a working mother, and although she made a point to be home for dinner—one of the reasons my parents bought their house was because it was fairly close to her law office—she also raised us to be as independent and resourceful as possible. And she encouraged us to help ourselves in the kitchen.

When you have two giant teenagers, you need food, and my parents had a giant freezer in the garage. They subscribed to a food service that would fill the freezer up with meat, poultry, seafood, and some veggies. The amount of food supplied to us was intended to last a "normal" family six months. But between Geoff and I, it would last three months, which meant my parents had to cough up the remaining payments before we could reorder. When Geoff left to go to Oregon, it took me and Mom and Dad about four and a half months to finish off the food. And once Geoff and I were both out of the house, the service threatened to cut my parents off because they weren't ordering enough. That's gratitude for you!

So I had encouragement, and I had access. The last element I needed to drive me into the kitchen was inspiration. Enter the Food Network. To me it was the most relevant channel on TV, filled with useful, interesting programs—not filler stuff—about a subject that is close to my heart (and stomach).

One day I saw a Wolfgang Puck episode about making pizza, and it struck me that this was a fun, not too work-intensive dish. You spend maybe five minutes of work making the dough, and you knead it for about three more minutes. Then you let it sit and rise for two hours and then come back and work on it for five minutes more. In other words, it was something you could do without needing a huge amount of focus. Perfect for a teenager, right?

It became one of those things I tried and just got into.

I made pizzas. A lot of them. I would call up my friends from Pali and ask what their favorite toppings were, invite them over, and deliver a custom pizza for each of my buddies. I'm sure my friends thought it was awesome—free pizza for a teenager is pretty sweet—but I got something out of it, too. It was good training because with each of my mini-masterpieces, I got to see how different toppings went together, and from my friends' increasingly exotic requests I got new ideas for combinations. Now, years later and thanks to all that practice, I have the dough down. I am not a thick-crust fan, although I can understand the appeal of the heavier, Sicilian-based crusts you get in many pizzerias and, of course, in Chicago. To me the perfect crust is thin and crispy, with enough substance to hold the toppings without falling apart. It should not dominate the pizza, which can happen with thicker crusts.

What I enjoy most about making pizzas is that you can play around with the toppings. That is the creative part. You can use goat cheese as a base and then add another milder cheese to create blended sensations. You can experiment with vegetables and meats.

There are no secret recipes I'm working with. These are the basics: flour, cheese, tomatoes, olive oil, and imagination.

Then again, sometimes too much imagination can be a dangerous thing in the kitchen. Case in point: my brother is a huge shrimp fan. In fact, there is no doubt he's going to write about Shrimp Pasta before this book is done, if he hasn't already. That's one of his signature dishes. Unfortunately, shrimp was probably the key ingredient in our worst pizza ever. We used an olive oil base when instead we probably should have used a moister white sauce. With pizza, you need a hot oven to cook the dough, but high temperature meant the oil basically scorched and dried the shrimp. They were so shriveled up, you actually felt sorry for them. It is the one failed pizza attempt that I carry around with me. But what coaches say on the football field is equally true in the kitchen: no pain, no gain.

One of these days, I'll make a shrimp pizza for Geoff that will make him forget that first fiasco.

By the time I graduated from Pali, I had been picked twice as an All-State Underclassman and earned All-Western League and All-City honors as a junior. In my senior year, the honors just kept piling up: I won the CIR Los Angeles City Offensive Lineman of the Year, the Western Lineman of the Year, and PrepStar All-West Region honors, and the rating service Rivals listed me as the twenty-seventh best tackle in the country, while Scout.com listed me at twenty-third.

Meanwhile that other thing you do in high school—you know, going to class—went pretty well, too. I'm a competitive guy, and I like to excel whether I'm on the field, in the classroom, or in the kitchen. I don't want to waste my time or anyone else's. So my other senior-year achievement was landing on the principal's honor roll and dean's list, thanks to a 4.3 GPA.

I had scholarship offers from notable schools: Cal, Michigan, Stanford, Virginia, Tennessee, Oregon, and Washington. I guess I can thank Geoff for some of them. When he went through the college selection process, the whole family went along with him, which means I tagged along as he met with coaches and players and looked at the facilities. I'm three years younger than Geoff, but I had already caught up to him in size, so the coaches couldn't help but notice me. I was in ninth grade at the time, and immediately set off pings on the recruitment radar systems of some of the best football programs in the country.

You can't teach size, right?

When it came time for me to choose a school, Geoff was great. He loved Oregon and had really grown with the program, but he didn't pressure me at all. In the end, it was a tough decision between Cal-Berkeley and Stanford that suddenly got easier when Stanford dismissed Coach Walt Harris. The new coach—some guy named Jim Harbaugh—called me to introduce himself. Of course now, having built winning programs at Stanford and with the San Francisco 49ers, Harbaugh is considered one of the great coaches around, but back in 2006–07 he wasn't a household name. So faced with the unknown coach and coaching staff at Stanford versus the coaches I had met at Cal-Berkeley, I went with Cal. It had pretty much everything I wanted. It's an excellent school, academically speaking. I really liked the coaches—from Ron Gould, the running back coach who recruited me, to head coach Jeff Tedford, to the offensive line coach Jim Michalczik. They spoke of a program that was dedicated to being both supportive and successful, and I could see that when I visited. Plus, in the back of my mind, I knew going pro was a real possibility. My brother was a serious NFL prospect, and he'd been telling me for years that my size and agility made me a perfect tackle. So I wanted a program that played an offensive style that would help me get ready for the pros. Cal seemed to place a good number of guys in the NFL, so that was a major factor. And the school wasn't too far from L.A., so I could drive down or hop on a plane without too much trouble. It was a perfect fit.

Looking back now, I can see that my father and my brother had demonstrated good foresight when they tricked me into playing football.

I still think I might have been a good high school quarterback, though.

At my size, I would have been a pretty tough sack.

4

DOUBLE MAJORS

Geoff

Going up to Eugene, Oregon, as an eighteen-year-old kid was exciting.

And intimidating.

I was a raw player coming in as part of a class of six offensive linemen, including a five-star recruit, Aaron Klovis, who was supposed to be one of the best linemen in the nation. I thought it spoke really well of the team that we landed him. But with top-line talent like that, I didn't have a lot of expectations for myself. I was coming in with a huge learning curve, too, since my high school team was pretty laid-back;

we didn't have two-a-day practices, we didn't lift weights, we never watched film. In comparison with some of the other guys, I was like a sub-rookie.

Also, I was still stuttering back then. I always had a positive attitude. But it is tough for stutterers when they find themselves in a new situation and stammer. It can be a little embarrassing. Actually, "little" is the wrong word. It can be totally embarrassing and brutally painful. My heart goes out to all stutterers. I can remember instances when I felt totally inadequate, like I wasn't normal, like I was cursed. And sometimes, looking back at being an athlete where so much focus is on speed and efficiency, I can't help wondering if my stutter appeared to be even more of a handicap. When the stutter took over, I was slower at communicating.

Fortunately, my positive approach and low expectations combined with the excitement and freedom of being in a great college trounced any anxieties I had.

Seizing the moment, I went up to school four weeks before preseason training started with another offensive line recruit from L.A., Jacob Hucko. We rented a room in a frat house, drove to the facility, and worked out with the upperclassmen. Those first workouts were intimidating. I'd never lifted weights before. I was this big guy who looked strong, but, in comparison to the rest of the team, was probably the weakest guy on the offensive line.

But I hung in there and watched and listened and started working with strength coaches to improve my conditioning and build muscle. Looking back, I'm glad Jake and I went up.

Nowadays, all freshmen start earlier. They go up for transition programs. We were smart enough to figure that out ourselves.

Plus, Jacob and I were eighteen-year-olds and in an awesome college town. It was the first time I was away from my parents, so I was into just having fun, going out, exploring the town, and being independent. Or semi-independent.

There was one other attraction for going up early that summer. Baseball. About a two-hour drive away, just outside of Portland, was a team called the Aloha Knights, of the West Coast Collegiate Baseball League, which is a one of the top summer leagues for college players. It's a wooden-bat league, so it's serious about grooming players for the major leagues. In fact, by the 2013 season, at least twenty players from WCCBL had made it up to the major leagues, with dozens more in the minors. The Knights—they now play in Corvallis and are called the Corvallis Knights—were sponsored by Penny Knight, the wife of Nike CEO Phil Knight, and they invited me to play with them.

It was a serious team and I was pumped to compete against top collegiate players. I ended up getting in one game, and it started like a fairy tale, with me nervously taking the mound and just zipping the ball in there. I got the first two batters out, and I thought, "Wow! I can do this!"

Then it morphed into a nightmare. Three runs later, I got the third out, and that was it for my baseball career. My ERA, I'm disgusted to say, was 27.00.

But you know what? The Knights won the summer league

national championship that year. And Penny Knight actually gave me an NBC World Series ring, so it was a bit of a fairy tale after all.

The luck continued—sort of—when preseason rolled around. For the initial practices they split offensive linemen into two groups: the older guys and the freshmen. But on the third day, they needed one more lineman to practice with the varsity. We drew straws and I won. So now I'm the inexperienced freshman playing with the established vets. I held my own that day, and from then on I would practice with the group of older guys who were getting ready to play the season, not with all the guys who were redshirting.

The season started with me on the team, but not getting into any games. I probably didn't help my standing on the depth chart when I approached my offensive line coach Neal Zoumboukos before the third game of the season and said, "Coach, I'm not getting in games, and Yom Kippur, the holiest day of the year, is on Saturday. So I'd like to take the day off." Neal is a Greek Orthodox, and he understands the idea of different religions using different calendars, since his own faith follows the Julian calendar. The Jewish calendar operates on the lunar calendar, so our religious holidays fall on different days of the modern—or Gregorian—calendar every year. He seemed totally cool with it. But I heard back that other coaches asked if this was going to happen every year, which I thought was kind of surprising. I guess it just goes to show you how rare Jewish football players are.

I finally got to play during our fifth game of the season,

an offensive shoot-out against Washington State. They called my name, I went in, and it was exactly what you hear about: trial by fire. Honestly, I didn't even get in my stance before the first play went off. I didn't know what was going on! The second play was a bit better—I blocked the guy I was supposed to block. And in the third play, we actually scored a touchdown. I was pumped. This was exactly what I came to Oregon to do: to play, to battle and win my assignment, to drive the team downfield and win, which is exactly what we did that day, pulling out a 41-38 victory. As the season went on, things on the field got much easier.

The pace of the game—the blistering, everything-exploding-at-once intensity—slowed down, as they say. It never actually slows down, though. You just get used to it.

Notice I said I was "sort of" lucky to play with the veterans my freshman year? That's because, knowing what I know now, I have to wonder what the coaching staff under Mike Bellotti was thinking by letting me play as a true freshman. The reality is I ended up playing in four games and about 80 downs my first year. Sure, it was a cool experience—it gave me a lot of confidence to be ranked high. But as a true freshman you want to get significant playing time, otherwise it makes more sense to redshirt, which is the term for having a scholarship player sit out a year without using his NCAA eligibility. While I suppose it is an honor to have been one of only three true freshmen offensive linemen over a twenty-five-year period at Oregon to actually play, looking back on it, I sacrificed a year of eligibility for a handful of mostly meaningless plays. Seriously, 80 downs is basically what you might play in a game. In fact, the next year, against Arizona State I was on the field for *100 plays!*

Everything has worked out very well for me, but it hasn't been easy. Sometimes I wonder how much better I would have been, how much stronger I would have become, and how those improvements might have affected my NFL draft stock if I had redshirted.

And I'm not the only one who wonders about it. After that first season was over, my offensive line coach Zoomer— Neal Zoumboukos—apologized about not redshirting me. In fact, he *still* apologizes to me every time I see him.

One last thing about redshirting: These days, college teams are filled with true freshmen linemen on the roster. That's because of two things. The first is that more high schools are running college offensives and have incorpo- rated college-like weight programs, so kids come in with more training and the linemen come in stronger and ready to go. The second is that it's a lot cheaper to keep a stu- dent athlete around for four years instead of five. I'm sure there are programs that have done the math on this. Red- shirting six offensive linemen every year must cost teams hundreds of thousands of dollars in tuition and room and board.

The only other issue I had with my coaches was this perception that I lacked aggression. They would get on me and tell me to be more aggressive. To hit harder, to want it more. This rap against me was hard to shake. You can go online and read pre-draft scouting reports, and there it is on cbssports.com: *"Lacks an internal fire and isn't an aggressive player."* I really don't know where this came from, this idea that I'm not as fiery or fierce as the other guys. Personally, I always thought it was BS. Sure, I'm from L.A. and I'm pretty laid-back and calm. And, yes, it is true that when we were kids, our parents were concerned that, because of our size and strength, Mitch and I might clobber our friends in a playful scuffle. So they taught us to exercise extreme patience and care to avoid fighting. I actually remember my mom and dad telling me that I had to act older than I was because I looked much older. All of that is true. Still, when it comes time to play, I'm out there fighting and battling 110 percent. And when it comes to practice, I'm out there drilling my butt off.

I can't help thinking that my stutter might have played into this bogus impression that I was passive on the field. Stuttering, after all, can come off as timid, which is the opposite of aggressive, right? You aren't rushing out words, you're not being verbally decisive, because, for whatever reason, you can't. The words just get stuck. But that's not because you lack aggression or desire. The fact is, I can actually remember plenty of times when I was afraid to speak up because I was afraid to stutter. So I wonder if coaches interpreted this as a lack of physical aggression and desire. I think there's a good chance that this came across during the recruiting process or the early practices with the Ducks. There were times I kept my mouth shut, and times I appeared hesitant or meek because the words didn't just pour out. I wish I had realized all this back then, but it's good to look back and understand where this might have come from.

Why did I stutter? Nobody really knows what causes it. Apparently up to 5 percent of children stutter at some point in their life. Most grow out of it. For the ones who don't, there are basically three schools of thought about what causes this disability. The first is neurological, that is, the brains of stutterers are different when it comes to speech. The second is that it's a learned behavior that sort of snowballs. If a child learning to talk stumbles and is admonished or criticized or punished, that response may breed more anxiety. The third theory is that stuttering is a psychological problem that can be treated with therapy.

I don't know what the underlying reason was for my stutter. But, as I mentioned earlier, it pretty much completely disappeared during my sophomore year. I'm sure amateur psychologists out there will note that that was the year I became a starter for the Ducks. Maybe that's what cured me. Who knows?

Other than the redshirting issue, I loved my time at Eugene and playing for the Ducks. College is a once-in-a-lifetime event for anyone lucky enough to go. Now that I'm married and have a son, it's fun to look back on that time. I cherish the independence, the freedom, and the support. It's really a laboratory for transitioning to adulthood. I was always a responsible kid in high school, but college is the first place where I got to be a somewhat independent person, managing my time, my work, and my freedom.

Being a student athlete is a particularly intense collegiate experience. It's fun, but it is focused. The four other linemen I came in with—I know we started as a group of six, but the five-star recruit eventually transferred out—all turned into terrific friends. We—Jeff Kendall, Mark Lewis, Jake, and Max Unger, who has gone on to great things with the Seattle Seahawks and the New Orleans Saints—all stay in touch and see one another whenever we can, going to one another's weddings, getting away for trips to Vegas. I should also include my defensive line buddy Dave Faaeteete, who I roomed with for years. We just have a blast whenever we get together. It stands to reason we would, since we spent huge amounts of time together, sharing hundreds of hours training, eating, hanging out and, ultimately, functioning as this super-efficient five-headed battalion specifically honed to go out and pummel other guys. We had pride in our accomplishments, individually and together, and we still do.

One of the things my offensive line teammates and I would do during the season was go to this out-of-the-way pizza joint in Eugene after every home game. We'd hit the showers and then go join our families, if they were in town for the games. The pizza was never that good, but the beer and pies were cheap. And anyway, it wasn't about the meal, really. It was a great way for us to celebrate, meet the families of our friends, and also have our parents make connections. My mom and dad are very social people, and I know they loved connecting with other supporters during all the hours when they were waiting for games to start.

The workload for a student athlete is extremely time-consuming. I remember seeing people on nice days just hanging out, relaxing outside the Erb Memorial student union, and thinking, "Man, I always have to be somewhere." The NCAA has rules about limiting the amount of time a student can practice, but it's hard to track. For instance, we were allowed to practice twenty hours each week during the season, but a game counted for three hours. But if you factor in the pregame meetings, and the warm-ups, and the travel to and from games, you are talking about a lot more than three hours. It's the same issue with training sessions—you have to ice down and shower, which can take an hour every day, but that's off the clock.

One of the perks of playing football was the food that was available to us. The massive spreads laid out at practice facilities are known as training tables, and they are the lifeblood of a football team. I ate so much during college, it was nuts. A lot of my eating was due to youthful ignorance; I thought I was working out so much and getting so much stronger that I could eat anything. So I did. I'm a rice maniac, and I would have bowls and bowls of the stuff, along with steak, chicken dishes, fish, whatever was on the table. And there was *always* food on the table.

My first year I weighed 355 pounds at one point, although

by the end of the season I was down to 330. My sophomore year I was 370, which was insane for my 6'6" frame. Not that it stopped me from playing—I started all 12 games at right tackle, gave up 3 sacks the entire year, and during our big rivalry game against Oregon State I was named co-offensive player of the week. I had made major contributions to the tenth-ranked team in the nation. But I knew I was still too heavy to improve my quickness. So I began a career-long battle to maintain my weight. It's a war that I've fought now for many years. At certain points I've even traveled with a scale to make sure extra weight wasn't creeping up on me. I don't do that anymore, because over the last four years I've finally fully understood how my body metabolizes food and how to properly manage my diet. But back at Oregon I didn't really know how to lose weight in a focused manner, and being a self-conscious kid, I didn't ask the trainers for advice, either. The winter of my sophomore year, I'd go to school, go to practice, and lift weights. Then I'd come home and do extra cardio at the gym in my apartment building, eat something, and hit the books. Studying is pretty much limited to nights when you are a student athlete. There's not a lot of time to get to the library during the day when you are at the practice facility from two to eight o'clock while the season is in full swing.

Eventually, I got my weight down to 345 for my junior year, which turned out to be a smart move because during the middle of preseason camp, my lower back started killing me. I had a herniated disc and I'm sure the excess weight would not have helped my mobility. There's never a good time to have a herniated disc, but junior year is when NFL scouts start seriously tracking most linemen. So I sucked it up and played injured for the entire season, missing only one game. We led the Pac-10 in rushing offense for the first time since 1955. But I have to admit, it wasn't a standout year for me. I had surgery on the disc immediately after the season ended. After a few weeks of rest, I began rehabbing my back. I didn't work out with the team during spring practice; I just focused on my conditioning and getting the muscle strength and flexibility back.

I also spent some time finishing my classes. One of the things about being committed to the team is that you spend most of the summer working out. I used my summers to take four-week courses and fulfill the school's math requirements. That meant by the end of my junior year, I had taken enough courses to graduate, which was something I'm proud of. My buddies who redshirted had a whole extra year to complete their coursework. The NCAA tracks the graduation success rate of students who graduate in six years or less. I had done it in three years, with only my political science thesis to deliver in the fall of my senior year.

How did I wind up studying poli-sci? Originally, I had planned to study history, but at the end of my freshman year I took an environmental history course that really wasn't much fun. It was a lot of reading and the professor turned me off to the whole history track. I decided to focus on political science partly so I could apply some of my history credits toward it, but mostly because I found I enjoyed the more theoretical aspects of it. It's not as cut-and-dried as history is; you get to voice your own theories and opinions, and you get to debate, which is something I really liked.

Going into my senior year, I was feeling good about my future. My back had healed. My schoolwork was done. And agents were calling, which was amazing to me. For years since high school, I knew I might have the size to make it as a pro, but I was never sure if I would be viewed as having the skills that were required. Now, it was looking like I had a real shot at getting drafted for the NFL. I asked my dad, who as a business consultant was far more savvy than I was about the negotiation process, to vet the agents that approached me. He talked to three or four and gave me his feedback.

The other great thing about my senior year was that we had a great new offensive coordinator who shook things up a bit. You've probably heard of him by now, but before Chip Kelly went on to become an NFL head coach, most recently of the San Francisco 49ers, and before he became the Ducks head coach in 2009, he was the mastermind who had turned his teams at the University of New Hampshire into offensive juggernauts that averaged over 400 yards a game.

I have to admit when Coach Kelly first got to Oregon, a lot of us were skeptical about his résumé and his ability because New Hampshire didn't play in a top-tier football conference. So when he came in and talked this big game about his no-huddle and the type of attitude and offensive plays we were going to run, we were all pretty damn excited to do something different, but we didn't know if it was going to work for us. Then we started practicing and we saw it in action, and we became believers pretty quick.

One thing that struck me about Coach Kelly's time as offensive coordinator was his confidence level. I had never been around a coach—at least not in college—who was as positive as he was. He had a way of getting us fired up and confident, and I think that confidence helped us play really fast.

The turnaround was dramatic. Coming off of a 7–6 season, we finished the year with a 9–4 record and were ranked twenty-third in AP's national poll. Our QB Dennis Dixon put up numbers that made him a Heisman Trophy contender (he finished fifth in the voting). Our running back Jonathan Stewart had some monster games, churning out more than 250 yards per game twice, including our final game—a 56-21 thumping of South Florida on New Year's Eve in the Sun Bowl.

Toward the end of that season, we were actually on track to play Louisiana State University in the BCS Championship game. But Dennis got hurt and our ranking plummeted. I will always believe we were good enough to beat LSU. Seven or eight Ducks on our offense made it to the NFL, plus another handful on defense. No Oregon team can say that, even all these years later.

Although we didn't make it to the championship, the Sun Bowl blowout was a great way to end the year and my collegiate career. Most of my buddies would be staying on for one more year, but I was done. I was free to hire an agent, and the day after the Sun Bowl, I signed with Deryk Gilmore of Priority Sports. I'd known Deryk for about five years; he ran the recruiting program for Oregon when I was a high school senior, and I knew he was a smart, creative guy. One year he created a comic book and would send out a page a week to all the recruits. It was a slick, full-color production, but it was too innovative for the NCAA. They saw the pitches and banned full-color solicitations, I think on the grounds that not every program could afford them.

Anyway, Deryk left UO after my second year to become an agent, and we hit it off. He's a great guy—totally focused, creative, and supportive. After I signed, he arranged for me to go to Nashville and start training for the NFL combine, where collegiate players are evaluated for the draft. The dream of playing professional football finally seemed within my grasp.

But I was worried—really worried. I had a major issue that I had been keeping secret. Something I would lie awake thinking about, wondering if it would hold me back, or even crush my dreams.

Mitch

Being a younger brother has a lot of advantages. One of those advantages was watching my older brother waste his first year of eligibility only playing 80 downs. So I went up to Cal fully expecting to be redshirted my first year.

Even without knowing Geoff's experience, I was destined to sit out the year; the entire class of linemen—and we had a really impressive recruiting class for the offensive line—was redshirted. For me, it was a great move. As I mentioned, I didn't exactly come from a dominant high school program. Pali didn't even have an offensive line coach, so I was a raw player. This isn't false modesty here. I had never lifted weights because in baseball I was a pitcher and my dad didn't want us lifting. So not only was I the weakest offensive lineman, I was probably the weakest guy on the whole team with the possible exception of the kickers.

I went up to school the first week of July for the Summer Bridge program. It was designed for all students to get acclimated. But in retrospect, it might have been the biggest grind of my entire college career. We signed up for summer school, so all the freshmen football recruits would wake up at 8 a.m. and go work out. Then we'd go to class, which are intense because they cram fifteen weeks of material into six or eight weeks. Then we'd go back to the training facility for meetings. The evenings were spent coping with homework. We'd get sixty to eighty pages of reading per night, and we didn't have any time to study during the day because we were doing football stuff. I have to say, that was kind of a trial by fire for me. In comparison, the regular season and all the following semesters felt easier than the one that was supposed to "help" me adjust to being a student athlete. I suppose it taught me a lesson or two, the key one being that the secret to summer school for anyone on the Cal football team is to only take one class in the early session, and then stop, because the second session overlaps with the start of preseason practice. And that is a deadly combination.

Actually, I learned a lot that first year. I learned about weight training and increasing my strength. I also learned more about my position—how to move, what drills I should be working on to increase my mobility, how to improve my leverage, and just hand skills in general. Blocking, when you get down to it, is about physics. We apply force at different angles to an object, in my case a defensive end or a linebacker. It's not exactly a science, but there are elements of combat, there are combinations of moves, and there are different methods to explore.

The most fun part was just learning about football on a more sophisticated level. My high school team had a basic play-calling system. The college game was far more nuanced and intricate. I got to study all the different variables and possibilities and start factoring in situational strategy into our planning and preparation. For example, if your team is facing a third and long situation, what should we be expecting from the defense? Will they be blitzing? If so, from where? And how should we counter that, or exploit that behavior? The battle in the trenches may be physics, but the game itself is a bit of a chess match.

These were things I just never appreciated. Looking at film for the first time was also an eye-opener. In high school

I was lucky if someone filmed a game. In college they film everything: all the drills and all the scrimmage practices. The only thing they don't film is you warming up and stretching. We studied everything we did, analyzing our sessions after each practice. Everything was new to me, and I appreciated it all. I felt like I was learning a new sport, getting smarter, and growing stronger.

I'm lucky that I loved what I was doing, because being a student athlete is a grind. After the summer program, preseason practice starts. And that was my introduction to two-a-day workouts, which I'd avoided in high school. Two-a-days could be brutal, especially when you are in full pads. My offensive line coach used to say, "Take a nap between them, and then when you wake up it's a fresh new day, you're only doing one practice a day!" That was a little trick to make you look on the bright side, and I took it to heart.

After that first practice in a two-a-day, you go straight in the cold tub. That's the smart thing to do, because the cold reduces inflammation and helps your muscles recover faster. Then you have lunch and eat smart: carbs and protein and veggies to replace everything you've burned up. After that, you either take a nap or you just zone out and make sure to stay off your feet. It's all about the recovery, which is the main issue with two-a-days. You have about four hours to ice, or alternate ice and heat, and eat and rest. You are just trying to recuperate for the next round.

Then you come back, have meetings, and watch the film of the first practice. Then you get ready and practice again. It depends where you are in the training season, but sometimes the second practice is designed to be a total grind as the coaches are trying to increase your strength and stamina, so it really can test your physical and mental toughness.

Practices, as it happens, come in three flavors: full pads, where you wear a helmet, shoulder pads, and knee pads; shells, which are helmets, shoulder pads, and shorts; and spiders, which are helmets and a half-inch layer of padding, sort of the interior lining of shoulder pads.

Usually one of the two-a-day practices will be in full pads, with the other in shells. But for linemen, as long as you have shoulder pads on, you are going to be doing a lot of hitting. So a shells practice can be almost as exhausting as a full-pads workout, although, obviously, in shells no one is allowed to tackle. At Cal, full pads meant the offensive line could cut block—where you lead with your shoulder and try to cut a defender's legs from under him. But not every team practices and cuts in full pads—it's really up to the coach. I'm pretty sure no NFL teams allow cutting of any sort during practice. The only situation I could possibly imagine is in training camp during live reps doing short yardage or goal line. But in the NFL knees are sacred, and I can't see any coach ever allowing you to cut your own teammates.

Another aspect of practice I discovered was the tempo. If you are in full pads they specify the intensity of the practice. So when you play "thud" tempo, everything is at full speed, but you don't actually tackle ball carriers. You just "wrap them up," which means the defenders get in position and try to wrap the skill player with the ball up. But there's no actual hitting.

"Live" tempo is the real thing. There's hitting and tackling, but you've got to be careful in practice. Causing an injury in a non-game situation is the ultimate sin at any level of the game.

Playing Division 1 football is a year-round commitment. The first semester of the year runs through mid-December, unless you are lucky enough to play in a bowl game. The later the bowl game, the later you get to go home. So a lot of players don't get to spend Christmas with their families. That was always a big thing with guys on the team, trying to figure out how they could get home during the holiday. Depending on scheduled games, college football teams work during big holidays. On Thanksgiving, we'd practice in the morning. If a bowl game was three days after Christmas, we'd have some limited practice sessions during the holiday. It's a fact of life. Being Jewish, missing Christmas wasn't a big deal to me, but I did miss Hanukah and latke-frying sessions with Geoff.

After the season, players are only allowed to practice eight hours a week. So I'd just focus on fitness training for eight weeks until spring ball's fifteen practices started. When that ended we'd all go back to working out and studying for finals. So the only time we'd really have off as a football player is from about May 15 to Memorial Day. After that, it was back to voluntary workouts, which pretty much the entire team attended. And since I was there, and the scholarship program incentivizes you to take summer school—there's a series of ten checks given out throughout the year to cover expenses during the regular school year, but for extra summer checks you need to be in class to get them—I signed up for a six-week class. After that, I'd take a little break where I just trained and chilled for three weeks.

I have a lot of great culinary memories when it comes to my time at Cal. The training table at school was a fantasy come true for a guy like me. And you have to remember, starting out as the team weakling, I had some serious muscle building going on, so I needed all the protein and carbs I could get. Every workout was a high-intensity calorie-burning, muscle-making jamboree for me. And the training tables offered two dishes of everything: chicken, beef, fish, noodles, rice, potatoes, veggies. It was heaven.

One of the coolest things about playing at Cal—I've never really heard about this at other schools—was the weekly postgame tailgating party. Actually, they were all-game tailgating parties, but since the team was busy, you know, *playing* on the field, we'd swing by after we hit the showers. These tailgates were massive affairs engineered by the parents and relatives of the players. They all got together and rented a parking lot at the freshman football dorms. Families would show up and start cooking and booming music from their stereos. It was an international smorgasbord. We had a couple of Italian kickers and they'd cook Italian dishes. The families of Polynesian guys would cook pork dishes. There were a couple of games where some of the tailgaters didn't even go in to California Memorial Stadium and watch a down. They just stayed outside and roasted meats.

It was a cool event. Berkeley has always had a reputation as a hotbed of counterculture, but that kind of hippie-dippy living didn't cross over into the football team too much. I guess you could say tailgating was the football team's biggest communal moment. There would be tons of individual cookouts going on, but often the parents would set up a communal, 100-foot long makeshift table in the middle of the tailgate parking lot and everyone would put food out. It was like a giant upscale potluck for everyone.

Celebrities would sometimes show up, too. My dad met Joe Montana once, and other 49ers would sometimes visit. I remember the marching band would come down, which was cool. They are a part of the total game day experience, and they work their butts off, too. It's too bad that college bands get to watch our game and stoke up the crowd, but we never get to see their half-time show because we are in the locker room.

All in all, the postgame tailgate was a great way for parents to meet the players, who are really their kid's best friends. Plus, they get to meet other families and Golden Bear supporters. Some of the parents and boosters would meet up at away games, too. One couple, Rich and Gail Roll, who I think masterminded the Berkeley tailgates, had an RV for away games, and so I know my mom and dad used to meet up with them and tailgate at every single game out of their RV.

Now that I'm in the NFL, I think about how rare that kind of bonding is between players and family and friends. In the pros, that level of interaction is almost completely nonexistent. Families usually just hang out in the lobby outside a locker room or in some designated room near the locker rooms and wait for players to leave the locker room one by one. Some teams provide refreshments, but for the groups waiting, everyone seems self-contained. There's not nearly the same level of camaraderie and interaction.

In college you are more than a team, you are family. You train together, play together, study together, and live together. You also suffer together. In the off-season we would have 6:30 a.m. workouts, which is a brutal reality for your average college student. I meet people who claim they got through college never taking a class before 11 a.m., but we'd be up at 5:30 a.m. to make sure we were ready to go. Every Friday, my offensive line buddies would go to this Italian place and eat ridiculous amounts of food. Breakfast burritos, pancakes, waffles, corned beef hash, breakfast meats, the works. It was an off-season tradition, which helped cure the pain of waking up so damn early.

Some people compare football to religion for the devotion fans have for their teams. Well, for football players, as in religion, shared meals are a major bonding ritual.

With the exception of my junior year, my career at Cal was kind of storybook. After my redshirt year, I cracked the first team lineup in 2008, started all 13 games, and won the team award for the Most Improved Lineman. We finished with a 9–4 record and beat Miami in the Emerald Bowl.

I ended up starting all 51 games Cal played during my four years of eligibility. That was one game shy of the school record, which I would have tied, most probably, if we had received a bowl game bid my junior year. But unfortunately, that was Cal's first losing season (5–7) under Head Coach Jeff Tedford. That wasn't the only down side to the year. Late in the season, my lower back started hurting and I was sent for an MRI, which showed a herniated disc. I'm not sure if it was the exact same disc that Geoff injured during his junior year, but man, that was one thing I didn't want to have in common with my brother. I played through the injury, which didn't really impact my performance. And then, just like Geoff, I had back surgery in early January.

The first couple of weeks I was basically just lying down in bed. Walking is good exercise after back surgery. The things doctors and therapists tell you to avoid are bending, lifting, and turning—the BLT of back surgery.

During my senior year I lived with two kickers, Bryan Anger, Cal's awesome punter who got drafted in the third round by the Jacksonville Jaguars—one of highest draft picks ever for a punter—and Giorgio Tavecchio, our place kicker, who's been bouncing around the league, from training camp to training camp, but unfortunately hasn't made a roster. It was a really great year. Giorgio was born in Milan and is an adventurous chef. There are not that many people I know—

especially in college—who wanted to make work-intensive food like gnocchi, but Giorgio was up for it, and we made everything from scratch. He also talked me through a bunch of great Italian meals. I guess that was about as wild and crazy as I got in college. I was focused on the NFL. I even got a hold of some NFL tape of the best offensive linemen and spent a bunch of time studying the tape, looking for tricks of the trade.

I finished school with a degree in American Studies as well as Pac-10 all-academic honors. I was listed high on most of the preseason scouting reports as an NFL-caliber player. And I won the Brick Muller Award for Cal's Most Valuable Offensive Lineman for the third year in a row. I'm proud to report we finished the season with a winning record, although we muffed the Holiday Bowl, losing 21-10 to Texas.

When I think about the level of talent on Cal, I can't believe we didn't dominate more games. We had five guys drafted by the NFL my senior year besides myself: linebacker Mychal Kendricks, my roommate Bryan, receiver Marvin Jones, safety D. J. Campbell, and defensive end Trevor Guyton. That was more draftees than any other team in our division of the Pac-12 that year. Yet we always seemed to have more NFL talent than we had college success, which is hard to explain. The coaches were obviously doing something right to train us and send us off to have successful NFL careers. But the total team game fell short for some reason that I just cannot explain. I guess there are plenty of teams in college with this kind of unfulfilled potential. You see it in the NCAA March Madness tournament, over and over again. Remember 2015 and how Kentucky, the team stocked with four first-round NBA draft picks (and two second-rounders), couldn't beat a Wisconsin team with two guys who went in the first round? It's one of the mysteries of sports: how teamwork, smarts, luck, and timing can all conspire to beat raw physical talent.

As they say: on any given Sunday . . .

SECOND DOWN

5

THE CHOSEN ONES: GETTING DRAFTED

Geoff

I'm about to tell a really embarrassing story. How embarrassing? It's something I've only shared with two people in the world: my brother and my agent. I don't think I ever even told my dad, who has been so incredibly supportive. I just couldn't bring myself to tell him.

This is not one of those "Ha-ha! My fly was open on national TV" jackass-type stories. No, it's about how I almost screwed up my entire career.

I bet you can't wait.

In the second week of the season during my senior year

at Oregon, we were getting ready for a huge game with Michigan. (And I mean huge. They don't call the stadium in Ann Arbor the Big House for nothing; 100,000 people wound up stuffing themselves into the stands. It was insane.) I was doing my usual weight training. My wrists were bothering me, which is not great if you are working with free weights, obviously, because you have to grip barbells and wrists bear a lot of the stress. So I was bench-pressing with 225 pounds on the bar, which was a standard weight for me. I decided to lift using something called the suicide grip.

There's a very good reason it's called the suicide grip— you don't wrap your thumbs around the bar, you keep them underneath the bar. That means the bar can slip off your hands and onto your chest, or neck, or even head.

And that is exactly what happened to me. My hands were sweaty and in the middle of a lift, the barbell slipped and landed on my sternum.

There are no words to describe the pain. Honestly, pain is part of the game. This was a whole other level.

The guys that were spotting me lifted the bar off my chest, and as quick as I could, I got the hell out of there.

I didn't tell a soul what happened. Not the trainers, not the coaches, none of my buddies. Nobody. I was so embarrassed. I was ashamed, really.

A day later I was in such pain that my eyes teared up during practice. I'd never experienced anything close to this level of agony before. It was absolutely brutal. I had one of the trainers create a pad to put on my chest underneath my shoulder pads, so it was actually protecting me from the hard plastic of the pads. I needed it because when I got hit in the center of my chest, I could not breathe.

I'm pretty sure I must have cracked my sternum. It became bruised and swollen, which, I'm told, is often a telltale sign of a fracture, but maybe that's an old wives' tale. I sucked it up and, ironically, the game at Michigan was one of my best in college. I guess the adrenaline from playing in front of 109,733 helped. Our offense was just a machine that day, with our quarterback Dennis Dixon throwing for 292 yards and running for another 76. We won 39-7 and handed Michigan their worst defeat since 1968. Not that I'm bragging or anything.

As good as that victory felt, my chest was a mess. I couldn't bench-press for about four months without severe pain. I'd still do weight training—squat lifts, dead lifts, curls, leg work, and everything else—but I avoided the bench and prayed my sternum was healing.

Why am I making a big deal about this? Because at the NFL combine—where draft-ready collegiate players showcase for the NFL—there are two drills that are viewed as enormously important when it comes to evaluating offensive linemen: the 40-yard dash and the bench press. The bench press test is to see how many 225-pound presses you can do in one minute. I had gritted and bluffed my way through the season, playing really well in spite of the pain. But there's no bluffing at the combine; you are literally studied like a lab specimen.

Despite the worry I had about my injury and its impact on my draft status, that was the best campaign of my years in college. It also featured one of the funniest moments of my entire athletic life.

I've always been a fan of sports radio for the same reason I like political science—you can have interesting discussions and debates. It's fun, it's often entertaining, and I'm interested in hearing other people's analysis, even when it's a call-in show and I have no idea who the callers are. One of my favorite sports radio guys is Jim Rome, who used to be on ESPN, but is now on CBS Sports Radio. He's very much a West Coast radio guy. He is probably best known for his rants—long, passionate soliloquies that are funny, entertaining, and opinionated, which is, of course, sports radio's bread and butter.

He came to Oregon in 2007 when it looked like we were headed to the national championship game. First he interviewed Coach Bellotti. Then, after we beat USC, he had our quarterback Dennis Dixon and the running back Jonathan Stewart as guests. And Dennis and Jonathan did something classy during the interview—they got Rome to agree that if we beat ASU, he would have offensive linemen on the show. I really appreciated that. I mean, who ever interviews linemen? We don't have much cachet.

Sure enough, the Ducks beats ASU—which moved us way up in the national polls to fourth or fifth—and Rome invited three linemen on the show. I was a huge Rome fan, so I went on with Max Unger and Jeff Kendall. It was a giant thrill for me, since I'd been listening to Rome for forever and had turned Jeff and Max into fans. Jeff was the one chosen to perform a rant and he was just amazing. He rose to the occasion with a wild six-minute diatribe that touched on every Ducks football issue imaginable—how many rival programs failed to recruit us, how our kick-ass spread offense was blowing teams away, our dynamic Ducks defense. Along the way he threw down a declaration: "We will play in a national title game," and shared our motto, "Respect all, fear none." But all of that was just a warm-up for this:

"Jim, we're just a bunch of fat kids livin' a dream!"

Of course, Max and I just cracked up, and so did Jim Rome, who loved the line so much he replayed it and quoted it on subsequent shows. We stayed on the program after the rant and were thrilled that listeners kept e-mailing about how Jeff had walked the walk and talked the talk.

One of the things I love about Jeff's fat-kids line is that it is self-deprecatingly funny and honest; it skirts the line between intelligent trash talk and flat-out honesty. But I also like it because, at least for linemen, it's filled with knowing irony. The world may look at us as huge, beefy guys—just a bunch of fat kids—but we know we are also strong, dedicated athletes who subject ourselves to grueling workouts for a game we all love. And when you can bench-press 400 pounds, or do 20 reps of 250 and run 40 yards in five seconds, it really helps you transcend any fat-kid stereotypes.

My mom thought the line was so great she made up

T-shirts for the entire offensive line: *Fat kids livin' a dream.*
We were all happy to wear them.

In January of 2015, I went back on the Rome show and he
not only remembered Jeff's rant, but he had his producer dig
it up and played a snippet. It's still as funny—and as true—
as ever.

I was majorly stressed about the combine and my weight
lifting injury. Coming out of college, one of the questions
about me was my strength, and some evaluations apparently
said I didn't play as strong as I should. You could look it up:
he's not very tough or physical on the field. I hoped that pumping
out, say, 26 bench presses would help counteract concerns
about physicality—especially since 23 presses is considered
an acceptable number. But I had no idea how many I could do
with my injury.

I flew down to Nashville to begin workouts and get ready
for the combine. At the training facility there were about
fifteen other guys on the same mission. The first thing they
had us do was test our 40-yard dashes. My 40 was not bad
for my size. I was happy. But then we went to bench-press,
something I hadn't done in just over four months.

I did three.

I was miserable. I talked to the trainers and to Deryk. As
I said, the minimum goal for any offensive lineman in the
combine is about 23 presses. Obviously you want to do more,
but there are ways to interpret numbers so that 23 for one

guy is the equivalent of 25 for someone else. How does that logic work?

Well, one thing they look at is arm length. If you have long arms, you are moving the weights farther than someone with short arms. So for a guy like me with a big wingspan, that would be noted. My 23 reps would involve more lifting than a guy with short arms doing the same amount.

But there was no way we could explain away a number like three.

Instantly the bench press became the main focus of my training. Everything I did was based on trying to get my strength up. I worked on keeping my elbows close to my body to relieve stress on the shoulder, I built up hand and arm strength. I worked the scapula—aka the shoulder blades—which take on so much of the stress during a press.

I tried to stay positive through the training sessions and vanquish the memory of the foolish, idiotic use of the suicide grip. I also thought a lot about whether the bench press was really a good tool for evaluating offensive linemen. My conclusion? Not really. The fact is that the bench only measures half of a lineman's power, if that. Our legs, hips, and lower backs are just as important when it comes to exploding off the line of scrimmage and driving an opponent back. Sure, arm and shoulder strength are a huge piece of the package, but it seemed to me, and it still seems to me, that the bench press should not be *the* key metric for evaluating talent.

Of course, nobody at the combine was going to care about the theories of a twenty-one-year-old know-it-all who was clearly feeling defensive about his numbers. So I kept my mouth shut and told myself I was going to make it work, and I busted my butt. Slowly—too damn slowly for me—I improved. By the end of February, my strength had definitely come back and I could knock out about 18 presses in one go. Part of me was glad, the improvement made it clear to me that with more time, I could eventually put up a respectable number. But part of me was frustrated, because I was running out of time.

I wasn't the only one frustrated, it turns out. In going back over my memories of the combine years, my dad told me something he had never mentioned to me before—that about ten days before the combine Deryk told him that Priority Sports was seriously thinking about keeping me out of the combine. "His fast twitch muscle isn't where it needs to be, he's sort of sluggish," is how my dad remembers Deryk putting it. And my dad's reaction was pretty forceful:

"I said, 'Don't you dare do that. After all his work coming back from his junior-year injury, you will wreck him. You want him to sit out a drill, fine. But do not pull him out of this thing. You'll devastate him.'"

So everyone was tense. And of course, being frustrated and stressed going into the combine is exactly what you don't want to be. That's because the weeklong event is a study in physiological and psychological warfare. Maybe those terms are a little harsh, but my point is that NFL teams want to see how you're going to handle the stress of a three-day job interview that also requires you to perform physically at the highest level, usually with very little sleep. The entire schedule is set up to mess with your equilibrium. They purposely save most of the workouts for the end of the process because that's when you're the most stressed out and tired. During my combine, they sent all of the offensive linemen to do a quad test on a Cybex machine as soon as we arrived. That was before we had checked in and dropped off our bags. The first two days they wake you up early to do your medical, take your mental tests, and meet with teams. At 4 a.m. or 5 a.m. on the second day, they wake you up for a drug test. Then you have six or seven hours of medical exams. Then, later that day, you have to participate in the "meat market." You take off your shirt and walk up on stage in front of every single scout and coach in the NFL and weigh in. There are about three hundred people looking at your body and silently taking notes. It's pretty weird.

And why do they run it this way? Teams want to see how you handle the pressure. And by pressure, I'm talking about not just the game day stress or the physical stress, but all the additional crap that life brings: family emergencies, sick children who keep you up all night, girl trouble, peer pressure from your old friends to live large. All of that. Teams aren't just looking for a physical upside, they're also looking for a player who can be consistent and stay focused at all times. A true pro.

I had only one private interview during the combine. It

was with the Seattle Seahawks. Naturally I was nervous. To me it was the equivalent of a big date with the most awesome girl in the universe. I wanted to impress the hell out of them. Instead, they impressed the hell out of me. During the interview, head coach Mike Holmgren pulled up one of my game clips from Oregon. It was a game against a lesser team and he said, "It doesn't look like you're trying as hard here."

He was absolutely right. It wasn't as if I was getting beat, but I wasn't going 100 percent. It was right there on the tape: me, not being aggressive. Maybe that was the play that had scouts saying I wasn't that physical. I couldn't say anything except, "You're right." I didn't think they would notice stuff like that, but even if you're a lower-round pick, they have guys who are watching all your clips. They remember your college games better than you do. It was a hell of a lesson.

At the combine, Deryk and I put our heads together. There was no way we wanted to deliver a subpar performance. Even though I could do 18 presses, which, if you add it up, is about 4050 total pounds of lifting, it just wasn't a strong number in comparison to other linemen. We strategized about me skipping the bench press drill. Would this hurt my draft ranking? Would people wonder about my strength? There was no way to get inside the heads of the GMs and scouts who were evaluating me. Teams are going to take whatever information they get and use it the way they want to use it. A guy might have bad numbers in the combine, but if he has

ckle in the draft, which meant I was potentially a fourth-
-six-round pick. I was cool with that. Sure, everyone dreams
getting a big fat contract, but that was obviously a dream
o far for me. Just getting the opportunity to compete at
e next level would be a dream come true for me.

That year the NFL draft was a two-day affair; rounds
e and two were picked on the first day, and then third to
venth rounds were chosen the following day. The advice I
t from everyone ranged from "Don't watch the draft" to
ury your head in the sand" to "go to the movies" to "what-
er you do, make sure you don't watch the draft."

And I took that to heart. I went to a buddy's baseball game
the first day. But when I got home, I talked to Deryk
d found out that seven offensive tackles—an unheard of
mber—were taken in the first round. I said, "Sweet!"

We both figured I would probably move up in the rounds.
When day two of the draft rolled around, I threw every-
e's advice out the window. I felt like, "I'm gonna watch
e draft, because I'm going to get drafted higher than we
ought." And I sat down on the couch at 6 a.m. to watch the
oceedings in New York. When the third round finished,
name was not called.

Then the fourth round went by. My name was still not
led.

At this point I started to get frustrated for a couple of
sons. I saw guys drafted ahead of me that I knew, in my
nes, I was better than. That hurt. Also, the phone was not

amazing tape, a team might ignore his numb
My tape was pretty good, and except for
issue, I expected to perform well in the othe

It turned out I was right. I did a 5.36 in
and a 1.8 in the 10-yard dash and 4.79 in th
All respectable for a man of my size and w
leap and broad jump weren't exactly off the
are not premium offensive line skills eithe
result? Well, Joe Thomas, the perennial
was picked third overall in the 2007 dra
Mitch on the Browns, ran the 40 in 4.92 a
1.75. My shuttle was slightly faster than
clearly had a monster combine.

In the end, when it came time for the
sion, Deryk and I decided to skip the drill

It was a risky move.

Very risky, as it turned out.

One thing I love about Deryk and the
Sports—even if they considered keepir
combine—is there is never BS with the
sweet talk about how I could go in the firs
There was no blowing smoke. They are re
As draft day approached, Deryk and othe
Sports talked with scouts and GMs, loo
drafts, and compared my combine and
against other linemen expected to be in t
their assessments, I was the tenth to fifte

ringing at all, which was another bad sign. Normally, a player who is about to get picked get calls beforehand. Scouts call to see if the player is getting interest from other teams, or to make sure they have the right phone number, or to give him a heads-up that they are going to take him and to be on standby. But my phone was silent.

By this time my dad and uncle were watching with me and we were all kind of shell-shocked. I actually think my dad, who later called it the most grueling day of his life, was taking it harder than I was. He and my mom had planned a dinner celebration for family and friends at—where else?—El Torito up the block. I could see he was worried about that. I went outside and shot baskets with my uncle to try to take my mind off things. I can't lie, it was hard. I wondered if all this was the result of my stupid bench press accident and a fractured sternum that nobody knew about. I couldn't believe it.

Finally, just before the start of the fifth round, I got a call. It was the Carolina Panthers offensive line coach Dave Magazu, and he said the Panthers wanted to draft me, coming up in the fifth round. I let out a sigh of relief. But guess what? That turned out to be a wasted breath, because the fifth round came and went, and I was still on the board. So now I was beyond frustrated. I was in such a foul mood, I said, "Dad, cancel the party. I'm not in the mood. I can't celebrate being an undrafted free agent."

In the sixth round I started getting more phone calls,

and so did Deryk. People were expressing interest. But some of the calls weren't about drafting me, they were about recruiting me to sign on as an undrafted free agent. The only upside about those kinds of calls were that a player sometimes has the ability to choose the team he goes to, so he can land on a team where they need more help. That's the theory, anyway, and Deryk basically started working out a deal in principle to go to one specific team.

Then Carolina called again. "How do you feel about being drafted?" said the coach, John Fox.

"At this point, I don't even care," I said. It was a 100 percent in-the-moment honest answer. I felt totally humiliated. I was completely over the process. And I guess I was sort of preparing myself for becoming a free agent.

"Well, we drafted you."

All my disappointment, sadness, anger, and frustration vanished in a heartbeat. I might have been the 241st pick, eleven spots from the last guy, but *I was going to the NFL*! I'd get a contract and a signing bonus! The living room was filled with high-fives, hugs, and laughter. People started calling and e-mailing, and before I knew it, the party my dad had canceled was back on.

I had done it. The stupid bench press accident hadn't completely ruined my career. I can't tell you how relieved I was. Looking back, I can almost laugh about it now. But there were moments that day when I thought, man, one stupid training accident and I've screwed up my whole career. The whole dream, all my hard work, could have been wiped out. I'm sure the injury and my decision not to bench-press hurt my draft stock. It had to have.

That night at El Torito, the gathering was smaller than my high school graduation party, but it might have been more moving. Hanging out with twenty of my close family members and friends made for a wonderful evening. The drinks were flowing and so was the good cheer. Best of all, my grandfather Norman—my dad's dad and the guy who helped instill a love of sports in all of us—was there as well. Even though Mitch was still up at school, we had three generations of sports-crazy Schwartzes whooping it up that day. I think everyone was so worried about me getting passed over that, in the end, being a final-round pick seemed like a real victory.

It sure felt that way to me.

Mitch

My transition from college to the NFL was a lot different than Geoff's. Once again I benefited from his experience. As he learned new techniques and training methods, he would share them with me, usually over the phone. As he messed up—like with his devastating bench press accident—I knew exactly what not to do. I definitely cut down on suicide grips, I can tell you that! When it came to selecting an agent, my dad and I talked to a bunch of guys who were wooing me. But Deryk had really been on the level with Geoff, and

I'd heard about how hard he worked making sure Geoff had options when the draft didn't go as planned. So that was a pretty easy choice, and a smart one. It sure made doing this book together easier.

Even though we are brothers, and we share a lot of the same interests, evaluating our football careers is not exactly an apples-to-apples comparison. That's because I played my first two years of high school ball, while Geoff mostly sat or played some JV during his. I also benefited from a redshirt year in college. Geoff didn't. So in terms of the sheer amount of hours spent training and playing and practicing, I had accrued a lot more experience than Geoff had at the same pre-draft point in his career.

It is always an interesting question: what is the secret to success? Why is it that more brothers don't make it in professional sports if they have similar backgrounds? I've read that often younger siblings benefit from having older siblings who play sports, which makes a lot of sense; they are more inundated with a sport at the earliest possible age. Is it about nurture or nature? The author Malcolm Gladwell in his book *Outliers* has written that it takes 10,000 hours to become great at something. Actually, I'm not sure I agree, especially when it comes to athletics. Some guys just have superior genetics. Hey, look at me: I inherited size. I couldn't ever be a successful lineman if I was 5'10" and 170 pounds. No chance. I haven't added up all the hours I've spent training, but I'm sure both Geoff and I were way behind most other Division 1 players when we started. Let's say in college we spent two hours a day training or practicing for three hundred days a year—that's a lowball number. After four years, we've hit 2,400 hours. And me? I had five years at college, so right there, that's six hundred hours more than Geoff.

At any rate, by the time I started training for the NFL combine in January of 2012, my agent told me I was pinging pretty loud on the radar of a bunch of NFL teams.

I went down to Nashville and trained with a guy named Kurt Hester—the same guy who worked with Geoff—along with about fifteen other guys. It was unlike any other training I'd ever done. The training was more like track and field work than football.

What I remember most, and what Geoff and I both laugh about and scratch our heads over, is the 40-yard dash. The 40 is a big deal at the combine, which is a little odd, because unless they ran track in high school or college, most players have zero experience with the intricate science of sprinting. They've never learned a starting stance. They have no idea how to "fire out" and explode into the sprint. They don't examine the mechanics of their stride, or how their arms should move.

So it's an entirely new experience for players. We had to study and learn form and technique, which was cool. As an athlete interested in biomechanics and moving efficiently, I found it all pretty interesting.

But here's the irony about the 40-yard dash: you train intensely for a month and a half—sprinting, sprinting, and sprinting again—because you are told it is an important metric. And yet *if you are a linemen, you will never run a timed 40-yard dash again for the rest of your life.*

I'm serious. I don't do drills with skill position players, but as far as I know, there is nobody with a stopwatch timing sprints during preseason training. At least not for offensive linemen. So it seems odd that the 40-yard dash is treated like a sacred, all-important statistic. I can see it being important for skill position players and defensive players, but for the offensive line, other drills make a lot more sense to me. The short shuttle, for instance, which requires you to go five yards to your right, ten yards to your left, and five yards back, would seem like a far more valuable way to gauge a lineman's ability, since that drill is about moving and changing direction, which mimics some of what you do in a game.

My 40-yard sprints during an actual game have been few and far between. Linemen are more likely to have to run that far after an interception or fumble recovery than they are during a successful offensive play. And if you are relying on an offensive lineman to win a footrace, your team is in big trouble.

Maybe I'm discounting all these drills and metrics a little because, to be honest, my combine numbers were underwhelming. The fact is I'm better at actually playing the game than I am at working out. So I did 23 bench presses at 225 pounds, which is standard. I ran a 5.38 in the 40-yard dash, which was slow, and 4.87 in the shuttle. My vertical leap was passable for a big guy at 26.5 inches, not that I'll ever have to actually jump straight up in the air, except maybe to catch a deflected pass. But my broad jump was awful.

The test I apparently, allegedly, supposedly excelled on was the Wonderlic Cognitive Ability Test, a standardized test they give all the players. The Wonderlic consists of fifty questions to be answered in twelve minutes and is designed to evaluate aptitude for learning and problem solving ability. To me, it seemed like a lot of basic math and logic questions with a few others that seemed designed to test my ability at focusing on little details, such as spotting the differences between phrases that might seem identical at first look, but aren't.

I never got my results for the test, but it has been reported in a lot of places that I scored a 35. Some people make a big deal of this number, since the average score is 21 for NFL players. But when you think that Ryan Fitzpatrick, the Harvard-graduated journeyman QB who has played for about six teams, most recently the Jets, scored a 48, my score doesn't seem that off the charts.

Fortunately my college coach Jeff Tedford had some nice things to say about me, so even if I bombed the Wonderlic, any team interested in me would have known that I have some functional gray matter. "He's as smart as any linemen we've ever had here, any player for that matter that we've ever had here. For him to comprehend what he's doing like he's doing it and not make any mental mistakes, there are very few if any. He's a very intelligent guy."

That's always nice to hear from a coach.

There are plenty of other evaluations that happen during the combine. There are informal interviews, and if a team is really interested they'll request a formal interview in their hotel suite. There are a series of medical exams where you strip and the medical experts from each team can poke and prod your body. That might be the weirdest experience in the combine. Sure, the entire process is designed to let teams evaluate your athletic ability, but sitting on an examination table six different times so that reps from all thirty-two teams can see you, well, there's an element of being an exhibit or part of a cattle call. Like livestock traders looking at steer, teams want to see what we are made of, how big and healthy we are, and if we are worth the investment.

Maybe I was a great interview, or maybe teams really love that Wonderlic, or maybe, as Geoff says, I had great game tape, but a number of teams expressed serious interest in me. Looking back on it, I also think my 51-game streak of starting at Cal probably helped my reputation as well. I only missed one play during that streak, and it was because one of my cleats came off. There's a saying that durability is more important than ability. And there is certainly some truth to that. You may have explosive talent, but if your body breaks down too frequently—and I think the NBA's often-injured star Derrick Rose is a painful example of this—then it's hard to help your team. If you're healthy and you're on the field, you can be productive. If you're injured and on the sidelines, there's only so much you can do.

After the combine, a number of teams approached us.

The Cleveland Browns, the Atlanta Falcons, and the Kansas City Chiefs all sent their offensive line coaches out to Cal to conduct private workouts with me. They also flew me in to see the facilities and meet with other coaches. And I flew into Pittsburgh to meet with them. According to Deryk and Geoff, these were great signs that I was being considered as an early round pick. Teams generally don't fly in guys they view as candidates for the later rounds.

They broke the draft into three days in 2012. Although some published reports predicted I might go in the second round, Deryk and I kept our expectations low. I would have been happy to be a third rounder. And after what happened to Geoff, I wasn't counting on anything.

But there was very little drama. The second night of the draft began with the second-round picks, and we didn't have to wait long. The phone rang right after the second pick of the night. According to my dad, who was sitting in the room with my uncle and his family and the Weinsteins, I broke out in a big smile during the call and everyone knew exactly what was happening.

I hung up the phone and said, "That was Cleveland. They're going to take me with the fifth pick of the second round." I'm sure I tried to be low-key—that is sort of my style—as I said it. But as everyone started cheering and hugging, I was ecstatic and totally relieved. There was none of the agony that Geoff went through. I got lucky. I was drafted higher than expected, the thirty-seventh pick overall.

The next night we went out to dinner at one of my favorite

restaurants, a Brazilian all-you-can-eat place, with about fourteen people. Geoff was there and it was a great feeling, knowing we were both going be in the league, doing something we loved. When the bill came—and it must have been a pretty hefty tab—my dad grabbed it.

"No. Let me get this," Geoff said, reaching for his wallet and discovering, in a classic move, that his pockets were empty. "Oh, man. I left my wallet at home."

Everyone cracked up. We'd all heard this before. Not that Geoff isn't generous; he's totally giving. He always wants to have people over and feed them. But our uncle has been known to lovingly refer to Geoff as "Alan Harper"—the "fiscally conservative" character played by Jon Cryer in *Two and a Half Men*.

So my dad paid. I remember thinking, "Man, I'm about to sign a serious contract. Next time I can be the one to pay. How cool is that?"

6

LEARNING THE ROPES

Geoff

It's no secret rookies have steep learning curves. Mine started from the moment the Panthers drafted me. I had no idea where the team was located. Honestly, I thought they played in Raleigh. I didn't know Charlotte existed. I remember going to look it up about an hour after I got drafted.

The next things I learned were lessons about money and the NFL.

The salary structure for rookies is pretty much set in stone as far as base salary goes. It's all laid out in the collective bargaining agreement and is based on your place in the draft. The only wiggle room is around your signing bonus.

When negotiations were over, I remember Deryk calling me and saying, "I got you an extra two."

"That's great," I said. "An extra two grand is fantastic. It will totally come in handy."

"No," Deryk said, "two *hundred*."

I was the eleventh-to-last pick of the draft. My signing bonus was $42,600. That's better than a poke in the eye, but it's a far cry from the million-dollar deals that the guys in the first two rounds get. So the lesson I learned was that if I was ever going to make some serious NFL money, I'd have to become a starter and earn a big payday on my second contract or sign as a free agent somewhere.

Rookies drafted in the late rounds don't get a lot of money and we don't get a lot of time to shine in the spotlight, either. But that may have turned out to be a blessing in disguise. Before I got to the NFL, I figured there would be a lot of dog-eat-dog competition in training camp, with new guys fighting to take jobs and veterans fighting just as hard to keep them. But from my first days at camp, which were held at Wofford College in South Carolina, I didn't feel any negativity or nastiness from the veterans. They were totally cool with me. I suppose the fact that I was a seventh-round draft pick had a lot to do with it. Maybe the offensive line guys were nicer to me than they would have been if I had been a first-round draft pick. Or maybe they just knew that as a seventh rounder I had almost zero chance of making the squad, never mind actually winning a starting position.

Whatever the reason, they were a great group of linemen, and they definitely didn't abuse us rookies. Hazing in the NFL varies from team to team. I've heard of some coaches that wouldn't stand for any of it, while others see it as a good-natured rite of passage and a way to keep things loose. In Carolina, hazing, if you could even call it that, was mild—it was pretty much limited to singing in the dining hall and catering to veterans' food and drink whims—providing drinks, candy, chips, and whatever junk food the veterans wanted. And I had to pick up the check for a few meals.

Most of the singing happens in that dining hall, and I lived in total fear of being asked to sing. I was still a shy kid. And although I no longer stuttered like I used to, it was still a concern of mine. There were times during training camp I would get my food and go back and eat in my room to avoid any chance of getting called to sing.

All of which is to say the guys on the team were more mentors than evil rabble-rousers. Especially offensive tackle Jordan Gross and starting center Ryan Kalil. I learned a lot about being a pro from them. A lot of different things go into being a professional football player. You need to know how to prepare each week, both mentally and physically. You need to know how to watch film properly, and what tendencies to look for. You need to know how to take care of your body and how to balance things—how to work hard and also have fun at the same time. It's a long season, you can't be serious every moment of the day. You got to have some fun.

Jordan and Ryan were just awesome guys, and they have continued to have fun right up to the end of their time together. When Jordan announced his retirement in 2014, ending an eleven-year run with the Panthers, Ryan showed up with an improvised barbershop quartet and sang a lineman-centric version of "Happy Trails" at the press conference.

Happy trails to you, my aging, departing friend,
Happy trails to you, I can't believe it's the end,
No more cares about the spin or speed or bullrush, just try
    and not get fat while in retirement,
Happy trails to you, you'll be missed on third and 10.

That's called keeping it loose.

With the new collective bargaining agreement of 2011 one of the tried and true traditions of training camp vanished. I'm talking about two-a-day practices. I experienced them at Oregon, and when I first arrived at Carolina we had them, too, alternating between two-a-day and one-a-day practices, with no days off.

There are certain things you get used to in football. I'm now very disciplined about my food intake. I'm completely comfortable with weight training. I can watch tape for hours as if it's a film festival. But there was no getting used to two-a-days.

As much as it hurts to say, I actually believe that two-a-days were valuable practice tools. You are pushed to your limit. And the offensive line gets to refine the intricate ballet that starts with every hike, which is absolutely crucial. But two-a-days were brutal. At its most intense, a team's offensive and defensive linemen are throwing punches, grabbing, cutting, and generally knocking the crap out of one another for about four hours a day. That is a huge amount of hitting, over and over again. And even though practices are held in the morning and late afternoon, the weather was usually scorching in August. Offensive linemen all complain about being in pads every day at training camp, but doing that twice a day sends an intensely physical sport off the charts. It's a physical and mental grind like few others. At the end of that morning session you have to ice down, eat, and try to recover, because chances are the afternoon session is going to be harder.

These days, the league has done away with two-a-days. My brother has never experienced them in the NFL. As much as I sometimes hated being in pads and doing two-a-days, I can look back on them as a necessary evil. I think now that we have less padded practices, the line play is not always going to as refined. It's like anything else. If you don't practice as much, you are just not going to be as good.

I held my own that first camp, but eventually I was cut and

assigned to the practice squad. That means I trained as if I was going to play—going to every practice, doing all the lifts and training, acting as the scout team, and basically running the same drills as the starters—but I never dressed for a game or traveled with the team to away games. I stayed home and watched on TV.

It was hard at first. I remember thinking my first camp was pretty good and I told myself that I should have made the roster. But looking back on it, I was being overconfident. I needed another year to get stronger and smarter and become more of an NFL pro. I also needed to work on basics. In college, I played in a two-point stance, so learning to play from a three-point stance took me a little bit of time. I also needed to increase my strength to make sure my punches—where you get your hands into the defender and throw them off-balance—packed the necessary wallop. Plus, my sternum wasn't 100 percent healed that first year. Getting hit in the right—or maybe I should say, wrong—spot would unleash major agony.

One thing you always hear about pro football is this mantra about the speed of the game, the speed of the game, the speed of the game. To be honest, the speed surprised me more in college than it did in the pros. The difference between college and the pros is really about the uniformly excellent skill level in the NFL. In college you might come across two or three defensive ends that are NFL caliber in your entire four-year career. Once you hit the NFL, all the players perform at an elite level; the speed, strength, and skills just go up a notch. Or three.

So what is it that offensive linemen are really perfecting during training camp and all the endless practices?

Blocking.

You can write entire books on blocking—on the training, on the technique, on the different blocks, on the footwork, on the hand-fighting. It goes on and on. But basically, we work on two types of blocking: run and pass.

I like run blocking more than pass blocking for a number of reasons. The importance of pass blocking can't be overstated—you are protecting your team's number-one asset, the quarterback, and contributing to what are ideally going to be big yardage plays. But for a lineman, pass protection is a little like playing defense on offense. On pass plays our job is to keep our bodies between the rusher and the quarterback. How we do that is an awesome, exhausting battle royal, no question. But with run blocking, the lineman's job is more aggressive. Run play blocking is more execution oriented. It's usually more sophisticated than pass blocking in terms of who is moving where when. It's more of a syncopated multipart battle, where we try to dictate with raw power, speed, and skills.

There are many elements to blocking. A well-executed block is a perfectly coordinated ballet of biomechanics, with your feet, hips, hands, and head all working together to create or protect gaps off the line of scrimmage. But the key element is what we call the punch.

An offensive lineman punch is not really the same thing as a boxer's punch. In the run game, the punch is actually a simultaneous openhanded punch and grab. You're trying to grab the breastplate of the shoulder pads, which is in the middle of the pads. That's where you get the most control.

To gain that control, the punch has to be coordinated with your hip, because the hips are where you are generating your power—translating the force and momentum that starts with your legs. So the goal is to hit guys on your second step as you explode out of your stance. If you land a punch on your first step, you will not be as powerful, because you won't have the momentum to bring your hips through with your punch. The momentum that builds with a second or third step is going to deliver more force. And you keep driving with your legs to sustain that force.

There are other factors that get calibrated into run blocking. Leverage is a huge piece of the puzzle for some linemen. If you are able to come at an opponent from a lower angle, you are maximizing your force and minimizing his. Leverage is key in every play. Interestingly, the word *leverage* comes from the French verb *élever*, which means "to raise," but in run blocking it's about applying force—to the inside, the outside, or the middle of an opponent—in a way that opens up gaps for the runner.

Offensive linemen have a very wise saying passed on through generations that sums up the secrets of blocking: "Low man wins."

That said, I actually don't play very low because of my

size. Even in the world of massive linemen, I'm a big guy. Instead, I rely on having really big, strong hands. I try to tie up the other guy, or move him with, as the saying goes, my hips, hands, and hat. I don't actually ever hit a guy with my helmet, but that saying is really about alignment: focusing your head, hips, and hands to work together and hit a specific target or endpoint that controls the opposition and helps the play.

Endpoints—where you want to hit the defender for a certain run play—are the targets to achieve leverage. The targets and how you hit them depend on where the ball is supposed to go in a given play. That dictates a ton of decisions, and we spend our time honing the moves to put those decisions into action. If the play is going to an outside zone then you have to use your footwork and your hands to match that. So that is what we are all practicing, trying to get to that point to where we automatically know outside-zone play means wider footwork, having my hands here, my hips there, my head centered. Then I need to know where to apply pressure and where it is okay for my guy to beat me. For instance, if the play is going inside, I generally don't care if he beats me outside.

There are other types of blocks, from trap pull blocking, where the goal is to make contact with your shoulders or forearms, to cutting, where you drop down low and take a man down by "cutting" his legs out from under him.

At the end of the day, the offensive line can be totally dominant, but that doesn't guarantee success. We are also dependent on running backs doing the right thing and hitting the hole we've created. Sometimes we'll execute our blocks perfectly, but the back just does something else and gets stuffed at the line. That is frustrating for linemen. We think, "Did he have his eyes closed or what?" But then we shake it off, because backs are human, too, and everything is happening at lightning speed, and decisions get made in split seconds.

The reality is that even though we practice and drill and are elite athletes, rarely does a football play—run plays especially—work exactly as planned.

Pass blocking also relies on punching, but the punch isn't usually as forceful because you use less of your hips. In general, you are upright and backing up as soon as the play starts. The punch is used to disrupt the pass rusher, tie him up, latch on to him, or ward him off. You want to be between your man and the quarterback at all times, so the rules of leverage apply as you angle your feet, hips, hands, and head to keep your blocking assignment away from his target.

Linemen deploy all kinds of styles. Some guys punch two-handed, some guys punch one hand at a time. Some are grabbers—they have very strong upper bodies and they either hold on to a lineman's arm or they grab that breastplate and keep the rusher close. On short-yardage pass plays designed for the quarterback to release the ball quickly, a lineman—smaller, quicker guys, not me—might cut the rusher. The problem with cutting—and you've probably seen this happen in games—is that once you cut, you are no longer between your man and the quarterback. So, if that rusher recovers quickly, the quarterback is vulnerable if he holds on to the ball too long.

In-the-trenches pass blocking often evolves into hand fighting, where the punches and grabs are launched and deflected as both players engage in a series of super-fast punches and blocks. It's often an elbow-to-elbow face-off, with the offensive lineman trying to grab on to the defender and hold him in place, and the defender moving forward while parrying our grabs. It is a part martial art, part counter-punching drill, part ultimate fighting skirmish that lasts two to four seconds.

And then repeats.

The best move I made my rookie year didn't happen on the football field. A few weeks into off-season training, I went to a bar near the hotel called the Buckhead Saloon with some of the guys on the team. Utilizing my superior scouting skills, I noticed a gorgeous blonde who was out with a group of friends. I'm not the wiliest Casanova, as you might imagine—stuttering can really put a damper on chatting up gals, trust me—but I can be outgoing, and as a new guy in town, I knew I was going to have to make my own luck. Fortunately, even though this girl was a knockout, she seemed approachable.

I decided on the straightforward, just-the-facts approach. "My name is Geoff. I play for the Panthers."

I guess there are better pickup lines. But, hey, at least this one was respectful and honest. The Panthers connection didn't really impress her. She said, "Yeah, whatever. If you really like me you'll take me on a date."

We started talking and the conversation flowed easily. Her name was Meridith. She had a warm southern accent and dazzling smile. She was a medical assistant who was also going to school to finish her associate degree. Her plan was to become a nurse. My plan was to get to know her a lot better.

I asked her for her number, and after a lot of talking on the phone, we went on an official date to a Japanese restaurant called Ru San's. It was a great evening, one of those nights when you really connect and have fun and you think, wow, this is the start of something amazing and special. It was one meal that I did not focus on the food.

I like to joke that Meridith and I were a perfect match. I was young, broke, played football, and didn't have a car. She was a total babe, didn't know a lineman from a cornerback, and had wheels. I guess you could call me a romantic.

But joking aside, I did use her car as an excuse to see her more. I'd call and say, "I need to go to the grocery store, what are you doing?" Since then I've found out that Meridith wondered about my motives. She'd tell her friends, "This guy, he's really nice and cute and makes me laugh, but he makes me drive him everywhere!"

The more I got to know her, the more I wanted to spend time with her. By April, we got a small condo together. Charlotte started to feel a lot more like home. It was Meridith's town and I could see myself settling down there.

At that stage I didn't realize how rootless life in the NFL could be.

I also put down roots of a different sort in the off-season with another old flame: baseball. I was talking to my dad about staying fit and sane while I trained on my own.

"What do you want to do?" said my dad, who as a business consultant is something of a professional listener and problem solver.

"I don't know," I said. "I'm so focused on training right now. It's hard to get out of the mindset."

"Why don't you do some coaching?" he said.

"Coaching?"

"Baseball coaching. Help out at a high school. You could be a pitching coach."

It was a great idea. I was living out by South Carolina, and I Googled the nearest high school and came up with Fort Mill, which is about twenty-five miles from Charlotte. I called up the head coach, Brad Mercer, and explained who I was and my background and asked if I could work with the team. He said sure.

That year I spent almost every day of the off-season handling the varsity pitching staff. It was great to be out on the diamond and work with the kids. They were a good team and the whole vibe was great. I've been a volunteer coach for seven years now. My fourth year with them we won the upper state and lost in the state championship. We've put a bunch of guys on college teams, and I'm proud to say that two pitchers landed on Division 1 teams, and one just got drafted.

I played a lot better in my second-year preseason training camp. I was just more comfortable. I'd had a whole off-season working with our strength coaches. My sternum injury was completely healed. And with the older guys helping me out with my stance and my punches, the moves started to feel more automatic and natural. Practicing against the defensive starters, I was holding my own. In fact, sometimes, I was more than holding my own. I was opening up holes with the running attack and keeping those defensive ends away from the quarterback. And the coaches noticed.

There are thirty-two teams in the NFL. Each team has fifty-three players on the roster, which means there are 1696 active players during the season. And by the end of camp, I was one them. Not bad for a guy who didn't play a down in high school until his junior year and was a seventh-round pick.

In week fourteen, we were playing New England and at the end of the game our right tackle Jeff Otah came out with a knee injury. You never want to see a teammate injured. Ever. We all work so damn hard on conditioning and strengthening our bodies, and injuries just negate everything players work for as an individual and as a team. I came in for a couple of plays to finish the game, but didn't think much of it. But the next day, the offensive line coach tells me, "Jeff is out for the season, so you are starting."

Two years prior to this, Jeff had been the Panthers' number-one pick. I was their seventh-round pick along with Mackenzy Bernadeau. Now due to injuries, both Mackenzy and I were starting—against the Minnesota Vikings, who had the sixth-ranked defense in the league and a mighty 10–3 record to our struggling 5–8.

The game was on Sunday Night Football, which meant I'd be playing in prime time on national TV. The Panthers' coaching staff was understandably a little concerned about throwing a rookie up against these guys. They made some changes to give me some help—mostly some double-team support from the tight end—which was really nice. I wanted to stand and deliver on my own out there, but I wasn't about to say no to that. Hey, sometimes it takes a village to raise an offensive lineman.

Now that I was starting my first game, I became a "media story." And for the first time in my career, reporters came looking for me. I was a little nervous during my first interviews, but I made it through without embarrassing myself. My teammates did their best to keep things very loose with some comical abuse as photographers' flashes went off. Among the mocking commentary: a few "Nice haircut!" quips, and then one guy called out, "He's the next Anthony Muñoz!" He was being a bit sarcastic; Muñoz was an all-pro tackle for eleven years in a row, and is still considered one of the best in the history of the NFL.

I was completely amped at the start of the game, a cocktail of adrenaline and the nerves surging through my system. Nobody plays this game just to practice. We work pretty much all year-round to play on Sundays, and I hadn't played a game—a real, actual, regular-season game—in almost two years. And even though I was nervous and butterflies were fluttering at supersonic speeds in my gut, it also felt awesome. Nowhere else do you get that rush, that anxiety, the drama that comes with being on the field and facing off, man-versus-man, skill against skill, brute force against brute force, over and over again for about sixty battles. There is nothing like it.

I played well, but by the middle of the second quarter—after about four drives—I was totally exhausted. All the adrenaline had surged and gone. Of course, you just dig deeper in those moments, even though you feel like hooking up an IV of Gatorade might be a good idea. I sucked it up. In the end, our offensive really clicked and we erupted for three TDs in the final quarter. As debuts go, it was close to perfect: we won the game, announcer Cris Collinsworth gave me a shout-out by noting he hadn't had to mention my name once, and I had realized a dream: holding my own against a very good defensive team on national TV. Pretty cool for a twenty-three-year-old practice squad refugee.

I think confidence is a crucial part of success. But any athlete with half a brain has moments of uncertainty about their skill level in relation to their opponents. Well, maybe guys like LeBron James or Michael Jordan or Tom Brady don't. But I sure did, because the fact is, you never really know until you actually do it. And I had done it. That night I thought, "Yes! I can play in this league."

And it wasn't just a thought, it was a reality. I finished out the season as a starter.

The next year, 2010, was my second season on the active roster. I spent most of the off-season in Charlotte training at the facility and bracing myself to win the starting spot at right guard, a pretty big challenge, since I had played tackle from high school through college. But when training camp began, Jeff Otah, the right tackle who was injured, hadn't returned to camp, so I just stayed at right tackle.

Starting was great, but it was a rough season. Our starting quarterback Matt Moore was injured early on, and a rookie out of Notre Dame named Jimmy Clausen was handed the starting job. He ended up throwing 3 touchdown passes and 9 interceptions over 13 games. As those numbers indicate, our offense was pretty bad. Going into the bye week we were 0–5, and the head coach said, "Schwartz, you're playing right guard." So for the rest of the season I played that position. The switch was fairly easy. The last six or seven weeks, I felt like I could handle either position.

I have to hand it to my teammates on the line for keeping everything loose and as fun as possible. It's pretty harsh winding up on the losing side week after week.

Playing well on an individual level was important to me, not just because I'm competitive and driven to excel, but because I had plans and was starting to dream a bit. I bought a house outside of Charlotte. I saw it as an investment. It was affordable and in a good area. Things were going fabulously with Meridith. I figured we'd live there forever. I sold her on that life. I said, "We're never going to leave Charlotte. I'm going to sign a long-term deal with the Panthers and this is where we're going to settle down." I had started every game and played really well. Just one more year of solid play and I'd be able to command some serious money and a long-term contract. This little dream of mine seemed totally within my grasp.

I didn't realize that sometimes your body—and the mysterious ways of the NFL—can conspire against you.

Mitch

The Browns held a rookie minicamp in May of 2012 and, even though I'm a levelheaded guy, it was a tremendously exciting time for me. Playing in the NFL had been a dream since I was in high school—as I've said, that was part of my reason for going to Cal, they had a great record of getting guys ready for the NFL—and now I was finally here. I had two goals when I arrived at camp: prove to myself I had the skills to play in the league, and prove to my coaches I could do the job and become a starter. I really wanted to earn the trust of the coaching staff and show them that they made the right choice by drafting me. Coaches and GMs want their draft picks to do well. But, in general, no coach in the world is going to start you until they are sure you are the best guy for the job.

To develop that trust I focused on improving my technique and fundamentals over the five practices we had. I worked hard on my hand skills, my footwork, my stance. And judging from interviews head coach Pat Shurmur gave at the time, I seemed to make a good impression.

After rookie camp, we all got integrated into the off-season program with the veterans. But, just like freshmen in college, rookies have a learning curve. So we had more classes and more meetings than the veterans. They gave us a class in financial literacy, which was a nice surprise, as if the team or the league is in your corner and wants to help you. Most of the other meetings involved teaching us the offensive schemes. All told, we had about four to five hours of meetings and workouts every day.

Before my senior year at Cal, I decided to study tape of the best tackles in the NFL and implement some of their moves and see if they worked for me or not. Ironically, the first guy I zeroed in on was Joe. I remember being blown away by how graceful and easy he made everything look. Obviously, it's an illusion, that effortless quality, but it was something I wanted to emulate.

Surprisingly, meeting him at camp wasn't intimidating at all. He was very low-key and approachable right from day one. It may sound like a cliché, but having an experienced vet to bounce questions and ideas off of has been invaluable. It was also inspiring because I discovered we kind of view the game the same way. We have relatively similar styles of the way we approach the game in terms of preparation. So, having him around is great. Even now, when I've been in the league a while, there are still things I'm working on that I'll ask him about, or how he would handle a situation. He gives insightful advice.

Not only that, but he's helped me with my confidence. During August of training camp the *Cleveland Plain Dealer* wrote an article about me. Joe had some very kind words about me exceeding expectations and having all the tools. If there's one guy you want to hear that from—besides the coaches, of course—it's Joe Thomas.

I was also psyched to be on a team that clearly believed in the importance of my position. I'm biased, obviously, but there's an argument to be made that the offensive line is the most crucial group of players on the field. We don't get the glory that skill position players do, but the fact is the offensive line must control the game for a team to win. And we must protect the quarterback. Michael Lewis's book *The Blind Side*, which inspired the Oscar-winning Sandra Bullock movie of the same name, delves into this kind of thinking. Obviously, Lewis focuses on left tackle as being the "most important" position on the field, because the left tackle usually goes up against the opposition's best defensive rusher and protects the blind side—the side a right-handed quarterback can't see as he looks downfield to pass. Lewis has a point. And he quotes Ray Perkins, then the Tampa Bay Buccaneers' coach, explaining his—at the time, shocking— selection of a left tackle with the fourth pick of the draft in 1988. "We would have taken him if we had the first pick of the draft. I've changed my mind about the left tackle position. It's now a skill position because he lines up against more and more teams' best athlete, their right defensive end or linebacker."

I'm very glad that *The Blind Side* drew attention to offensive linemen, and while I understand how incredibly important the left tackle is, there is part of me that feels like it does a slight disservice to the rest of the offensive line. Your team could have the world's greatest left tackle and quarterback, or the world's best running back or receiver, but if the center or guards or the right tackle can't block or handle the pressure, that great talent will never get to shine. The QB will be sacked, the running backs tackled behind the line of scrimmage, and the receivers will barely have time to start a route, never mind catch a pass. So, yeah, the left tackle has a tough job. There's no arguing that. But the offensive line is a multiheaded organism, and everyone has to be rock solid, or the team will be in a jam. In this age of big data, I'd be interested to know how many quarterbacks have been sacked and knocked out of games from defensive headhunters coming in from the right side. I know in 2014, the NFL sack leader was Justin Houston of the Kansas City Chiefs. He plays left outside linebacker, which means he doesn't attack the blind side; he attacks my side. And guess who finished second in sacks? Left defensive end J. J. Watt of the Houston Texans. Look, I'm sure historically there's been more damage to quarterbacks from the blind side—I mean the whole blind side concept was crystalized by Lawrence Taylor playing right outside linebacker and delivering a ferocious, horrifying hit on Washington quarterback Joe Theismann that resulted in a gruesome career-ending compound fracture of the tibia and fibula for Joe. But I have to wonder if there isn't a huge difference in the pressure being generated from one side of the line and the other. Of course, now that I've put that in print, I'm sure some data-crunching statistician will be anxious to prove me wrong.

Arriving in the NFL, I thought the game moved a bit faster. But the big difference, to me, was the competition is more skilled than it was in college. For instance, we spend a lot of time focusing on hand fighting. We use our hands to deliver punches and knock the defense back at various angles to open holes or just protect our quarterback. So we work on delivering those hits in a fast and furious manner and making sure we keep our balance. Why is balance important? Because the defense also practices working their hands. So you might be able to get a really good punch on a guy, but if he's able to withstand it and grab your wrist, he might be able to pull you off balance. In college, most defensive linemen did not have that ability. So the skill level—the fact that every team has guys who are beasts—was really the biggest difference to me.

There are other big differences about being in the pros. Preseason games were a new experience and were invaluable in terms of getting me ready for the pros. During the college preseason, I just practiced against my teammates for an entire month. It can get a bit monotonous. I knew the defense's moves and tendencies. And, man, I ended up practicing against some of these guys for four or five years in a row. So preseason games were a nice twist.

Now that I'm a quasi-veteran, though, there is one aspect of the preseason games I don't relish, which is that there are guys on the other team who are fighting to make the roster, and the way they do that is by trying to kick my butt. I'm trying to beat them, too, but at this point, a preseason game is not life or death to me. I don't need to make a statement, but the other guys might.

Being a low-key, fairly shy guy, I was a little worried about rookie razzing coming into camp. Fortunately for me our head coach Pat Shurmur didn't like hazing of any kind. I know that with some coaches you can make rookies sing or carry a teddy bear or do what you want with their hair, but Coach Shurmur banned the whole thing, so I got off in terms of that. I still had rookie duties, though. I had to make sure the meeting room was ready at all times with coffee, cups, and individual items. If a guy liked a certain snack, I had to make sure they were taken care of. On road games I dropped a bundle paying for late-night pizzas.

With head coach, Mike Pettine, we had a bit more fun with the rookies. I've never been an instigator, but sometimes at the start of a team meeting one of the veterans will have a rookie stand up and sing. If you're in the cafeteria during lunch during training camp someone might demand a performance. It's not mean hazing or anything. There are times when people start cheering or even join in. And it sure breaks up the mood.

When preseason was over, I was named the starting right tackle. Our first game was against the Philadelphia Eagles and my assignment was to go up against Jason Babin, a Pro Bowl left defensive end coming off an 18-sack season. I was pretty nervous. It was a trial by fire for me. When you face a player for the first time, you've got to get a feel for how they play things, their speed, and their strength. These elements are there to see on film, but you never know how you are going to react until you have to deal with it on the field.

With Babin, it was a battle, and I'm sorry to say I didn't acquit myself particularly well. I knew from studying tape that he was a high-effort guy who was going to give everything he's got on every single play. Some defensive linemen vary their intensity; they turn it on and turn it off, and you are not sure what you are getting on every play. With a guy like Babin, you know he is coming as hard as he can on every down. That means you've got to bring it just as hard.

The first play of the game was a run to my side and I completely whiffed on hitting Babin, so that wasn't the most auspicious start. After that, I sort of held my own. He got by me for one sack and a couple of hits on our rookie quarterback, Brandon Weeden. When those things happen, I get pretty teed off at myself, but I strive to control my anger and I try to analyze how and why he got through. I try to remember the move and think about countering it the next time, or not even letting him make the move. On the positive side, I didn't draw a single penalty. I didn't want to get flagged and have TV announcers tag me with the standard "new guy gets the jitters and goes early to avoid getting beat at the line of scrimmage." So I stayed locked into moving at exactly the right time.

As uninspired as my play was, it had nothing on poor Brandon. He endured what may be one of the worst debuts in history, with 4 interceptions and 2 fumbles. I joke that at least I didn't have the worst day on the field. Even with both our rough debuts, we almost won the game. With about two minutes left on the clock, we were up 16 to 10. But Michael Vick led a drive that ended with a short TD pass to tie it up. And the extra point killed us.

It was a rough season. The Browns started 0–5 and ended up finishing at 5–11, which was one game better than the previous year. So I guess you could say we were moving in the right direction. On a personal level, I felt pretty good about my performance and contributions. I started every game and played every single offensive down—that's 982 snaps. The Pro Football Writers of America named me to their All-Rookie Team, which was nice. I was also part of an offensive line that helped Trent Richardson break a number of club rushing records for rookies, beating Cleveland legend Jim Brown's marks for rushing yardage and touchdowns.

That said, losing stinks. Like everyone else in the league, I hate it.

7

ROOKIES AND RELIGION

Mitch

Neither of us realized it at the time, but my arrival in the league was an historic event for ethnographically inclined students of the game. I don't know who researched the matter, but before I had even played my first game, someone decided to find out how many Jewish brothers had played together in the NFL. It turns out Geoff and I were the first fraternal "members of the tribe" to roam the fields of the NFL since Ralph and Arnold Horween played in 1923.

I guess I shouldn't have been surprised that someone would research this. Growing up, as huge sports fans and as

Jews, we were definitely aware of the few professional athletes who were Jewish. It was just common knowledge. Something you discover about a player because . . . well, there just aren't that many of us in the world of professional sports. According to the U.S. Census, Jews make up about 2.2 percent of the U.S. population. Assuming that metric is accurate, Jews as a demographic group are underrepresented in pro sports. That fact leads to a joke every Jewish kid knows: What's the shortest book ever written? *Jewish Sports Legends.*

I think it's good to be able to laugh at myself. Of course there have been some truly great Jewish athletes: Hank Greenberg and Al Rosen were former MVPs in baseball and Sandy Koufax may have been the most dominant pitcher in the history of the game. In swimming, Mark Spitz, Jason Lezak, and Dara Torres brought home plenty of Olympic gold medals. In boxing we were represented by two well-known sweet scientists: Max Baer, the former heavyweight world champ, and Barney Ross, who held three belts in lighter divisions. In basketball, Dolph Schayes was a major force in the '50s, along with Red Holzman, who went on to be a legendary coach of the New York Knicks.

Growing up in L.A., I knew about Sandy Koufax, and everyone in town new Shawn Green of the L.A. Dodgers was a member of the tribe. But I had no idea about the history of Jews and football.

It turns out that Ralph and Arnold Horween were major football stars. They were All-Americans at Harvard, where they starred in the backfield. They joined the Racine Cardinals of the fledgling Canton, Ohio-based American Professional Football Association and moved with the team when it became the Chicago Cardinals. Interestingly, they played using an Irish last name, McMahon. It is not clear to me exactly why they used an alias. I've read one theory that they wanted to protect the family name. But since the family name had been changed from Horowitz when they first arrived in the United States, you have to wonder what was going on there. Was football looked down upon? Was their family ashamed? Or were they concerned about anti-Semitism? I'm not sure what the motive was. The name game gets even stranger when you read the obituary notice for Ralph that ran in the *Chicago Tribune*—it mentions that Ralph was the first NFL player to live to be over one hundred years old— and discover that Ralph's two sons have the last name Stow. Were they his stepsons? That's another mystery.

As a guy who majored in American Studies, I had fun looking the Horweens up. They sound like great guys. They both withdrew from Harvard during World War I and enlisted in the Navy. Then they came back, finished school, won the Rose Bowl, and turned pro. Eventually Ralph went to Harvard Law School and became a patent lawyer, while Arnold ran the family business, the Horween Leather Company. And guess what? Their leather was used to make footballs for the fledgling league.

It was also cool to discover that Jews were no strangers to the NFL in the early days of the league. Many Jews were stars during the 1930s and '40s, and none was bigger than

Chicago Bears legendary quarterback and Hall of Famer Sid Luckman. In the modern era, I think Lyle Alzado might rank as the most famous football player with a Jewish heritage. When Geoff came into the league, there were ten or eleven Jewish guys playing, but that number has dropped. Off the top of my head, I can think of Gabe Carimi, an offensive lineman for the Atlanta Falcons, Nate Ebner, a safety/ defensive back for the New England Patriots, and Taylor Mays, a special teams guy for the Oakland Raiders. Five guys out of 1,600 active players in the league? That's about 0.3 percent. Numbers like that make me realize that Geoff and I are a rarity.

I don't think I quite understood how important it is to some people that there are Jews who are professional athletes. I'm starting to realize how big a thing it is in general. It makes sense; all ethnic groups are proud of their members' achievements. Geoff and I are members of an elite profession.

The first time it really hit me was when I drove to Canton, Ohio, to visit the Pro Football Hall of Fame one Friday. I had been in Cleveland a couple of weeks and I thought it would be cool to go check it out. Canton is only about a ninety-minute drive south of Cleveland. It was a great place to take in the history of what has become the most popular sport in America. When I came outside, there was a busload of Orthodox teenagers visiting from New York. Just like there are many denominations of Christians, there are all kinds of Jews. Orthodox Jews—and believe me, there are many different Orthodox sects—are extremely observant. The men keep their heads covered with yarmulkes or hats, and they pray numerous times a day. They believe that the Torah, or Old Testament, is God's law along with the Talmud. I was surprised to see the group there at the Hall of Fame.

And they were surprised that there was such a thing as a Jewish football player. When someone pointed me out to them, they flocked over and peppered me with questions, asking if I played quarterback, if I would pose for pictures, and if I would sign autographs. It was really strange for me, because I don't usually think of myself as a big name or a celebrity. But suddenly, at least to these kids, I was.

"I'm going to root for you every game," one kid told me. "Except when you play the Giants."

Geoff

When Mitch arrived in the league, we instantly accounted for at least 20 percent of all Jewish players in the NFL, or probably more. As my brother said, there seems to be between five to ten players in the league at any time. I suppose there are more Jews than there are Hindus and Buddhists, but I guess our numbers in the league and across America are low enough that it turns out a lot of players don't know much about the Jewish faith.

I enjoy sharing aspects of the culture I grew up with.

Coming from a Conservative Jewish family, I loved the traditions, the rituals, the lessons, and of course, the meals. They are totally part of me. I have been asked a lot of questions over the years. When I showed up in Oregon, one guy asked if my family celebrated Thanksgiving. I told him I was an American and that, yes, my family loves Thanksgiving, we celebrate it every year. I should have added that giving thanks is one of the things Jews do all the time in our prayers. Many Jews thank God for food and wine before meals, not unlike saying grace.

The other really common question people ask me is: "Do you get a present every night during Hanukah?" My answer is: "Yeah, I did when I was seven." But the fact is, Hanukah isn't the huge gift-giving event that Christmas is. Some families may treat it that way, but my family didn't.

Questions like that don't surprise me. If you've never come in contact with or studied a culture or religion, then how can you be expected to know much about it?

Still, ignorance and insensitivity can be shocking. During my second year at Oregon, a freshman performed a song during a rookie show that referenced "Jews burning in ovens." I think that some people don't really realize that the Holocaust is not something to joke about. Back then I was just disappointed that people can be so unaware and unfeeling.

Of course that is nothing compared to the story a Jewish friend of mine once told me. He was living in upstate New York when a casual acquaintance asked if it was true "about the checks."

"What are you talking about?" my friend asked.

"Do you really bury the dead with blank checks so they can buy their way into heaven?"

What do you say to something as ridiculous and nasty as that?

That kind of racist mythology and stereotyping is horrible and offensive. So I actively share the Jewish traditions I can with my teammates. During Hanukah I've traveled with a menorah and lit candles in the hotel room, once with a coach who was Jewish. As you know, Mitch and I are latke addicts. But latkes, as I've said, are work-intensive food because of all the peeling and grating. Recently I found a great recipe that takes the work out of latkes, so I can make huge batches for my teammates. The secret is using pre-sliced frozen hash browns. I can hear latke fans out there groaning in protest. Hey, I was skeptical, too. But this is a low-intensity latke workout. You defrost the hash browns, squeeze out the liquid, grate the onion, squeeze out that liquid too, mix it all together with the other ingredients, and fry it up. It's delicious. Mitch and I have both made them for holiday parties. And our teammates—many of whom have never seen or heard of a potato pancake—have scarfed them down.

As Mitch noted, there are all kinds of Jews. As I see it everyone in the world should be free to follow their own religious path. Being a professional football player, I have to miss some traditions and holidays. Do I want to miss them? No. While I did sit out Yom Kippur once during my freshman year in college when I wasn't making it into games, as a pro in the NFL I don't feel I have that option. There are 16 games in the regular season. Every game is just as important as the next so, if I'm healthy, I'm determined to play in every single one. It's what I get paid to do, and I have a commitment to my teammates and my family to excel at my job. Sitting on the sidelines or missing a game because of a holiday is just not an option for me.

But I do go to temple when I get the chance. It's important to me to honor tradition. Especially on the High Holy days, such as Yom Kippur, when you typically fast and reflect on your life and your actions. So if the holiday falls on the weekend, I try to make it work somehow. I've gone to services at the start of the holiday when it has fallen on Friday nights, but after that, I'm committed to the team and the upcoming game. It's tough, but I know I'll have my job for only a certain number of years, and I'll have the rest of my life to go to services.

When my dad grew up everyone knew the story of Sandy Koufax, the Dodger star pitcher who refused to pitch the first game of the 1965 World Series because it was Yom Kippur, the Day of Atonement that is considered the most holy day of the year. It was great that he did that, but comparing a baseball player sitting out a game to a football player sitting out is not an apples-to-apples comparison. There were plenty more games for Koufax to pitch. He started and lost game two, and went on to pitch—and win—the fifth and seventh games of the series.

When I asked my dad about Koufax, he had an interesting perspective. "I think in some ways Koufax made it worse for other Jewish players," he said. "When you're Koufax, and you've just won twenty-seven games, you can do what you want and no one says boo to you. But what if you're not a star? There's always going to be pressure to play."

My dad is right. Within the culture of football, it's hard to miss a game for religion—and it doesn't make it any easier when people don't understand the religion. But even if they do, it wouldn't make much difference. There is definitely pressure to play come game day in the NFL no matter what the issue. People play when they are hurt, they play when they are sick, they play when their kids are getting born, and when their parents are dying. It is a competitive game. And unless you are a star, like Sandy Koufax, everyone can be replaced. So I play, because I love it, because I want to contribute, and because it's my job.

I'm proud to be a role model to young Jewish kids and athletes, letting them know it's possible for them to reach their goals. Mitch and I were honored at a fund raiser for a Jewish charity dedicated to meeting the nonmedical needs of seriously ill children called Chai Lifeline in 2015, and the response of the community was humbling. We were told it was a record turnout. People wanted to pose for pictures with us, and they asked for our autographs. As Mitch says, it was surprising because neither of us ever thinks of ourselves as celebrities. But to the people in the audience—kids and adults—we were a point of pride. It felt great.

I do wish that Passover would occur during the season. I'd love to host a seder for my teammates. Eating with your teammates—and really, with anyone—is an ancient recipe for connecting. Unfortunately, the season is over by the time the holiday rolls around.

Growing up, the Passover seder was always one of my favorite meals of the year. Seder means "order or arrangement" in Hebrew. So it is really a ritual in which we gather at the dinner table and recount the miracles that brought Jews out of slavery in Egypt. We take turns reading passages about the story of Moses. It's always a jovial mood with kibitzing and jokes, that warm atmosphere comes with being around the people you love and are comfortable with. I think the mood is also helped by the fact you are supposed to drink four glasses of wine during the evening.

At the Weinsteins' house, where we'd celebrate every year, they'd keep the meal loose and interesting. Seders weren't just the strict reading of prayers and recounting of the story, which is important, because while you are sitting there reading, the smells of brisket and matzo ball soup are wafting around the house, making you hungrier and hungrier. They would have their sons sing the four questions, one of which asks, "Why is this night different from all other nights?" The answers are we recline—some people sit on cushions or pillows—during the meal to mark our freedom, we eat bitter herbs to remind us of slavery, we dip a vegetable into salt water to remind us of shed tears in Egypt, and we only eat matzo instead of leavened bread.

Because the seder is about thanking God for the libera-
tion of the Jews, sometimes we'd have conversations about
oppression and people of all faiths who live under modern-
day pharaohs, which, for me, sort of takes the holiday rooted
in the past and brings it into the present. I really liked that.
When we were younger, the parents would hide a ceremo-
nial piece of the matzo called the Afikomen and we would
have to find it, get a reward, and then share it as "dessert."

Our dad is one of the rare people on the planet who eats
matzo year-round. Mitch and I aren't big fans of the stuff.
We tend to view matzo as a bland, crunchy carbohydrate-
based food-delivery system. If you've never had matzo, imagine a giant saltine cracker without all that salt, and that will
give you some idea of what we're talking about. It's thin,
dry, and brittle unleavened bread.

Symbolically, of course, it's crucial to Passover—reminding
us that as our ancestors were fleeing through the desert
there was no time to wait for dough to rise. But speaking
from our own taste buds, it exists as a vessel for condiments,
like an apple, nuts, and wine concoction called charoset. And
of course, during the next eight days of the holiday we put
everything on it: peanut butter, butter and jam, cheese.

Speaking of Jewish meals, while I love our soul food—
latkes, hamentashen, blintzes, knishes, gefilte fish, matzo
ball soup, pastrami on rye—I was not raised in a kosher
household. I eat everything and so do many Jews. Frankly, it
would be extremely difficult, if not impossible, to observe
kosher laws and make your way through the NFL as a

340-pound lineman who needs to eat huge amounts of protein. Teams are understandably not going to cater to one person's religious dietary laws.

There have been instances where I've posted images of food on my Twitter feed and someone will invariably say, "That's not kosher!" This is not the response I'm looking for. I never said I was kosher. It is interesting that some people want me, or expect me, to mirror their behavior. Personally, I take a modern view of religion and laws. While some of the dietary laws made perfect sense to protect people from sicknesses such as trichinosis, which is transmitted through pork, and hepatitis, which can be transmitted through shellfish, modern health laws and improved sanitary food practices have pretty much eliminated the health reasons that I believe at least partially inspired these prohibitions.

THIRD DOWN

8

MY BROTHER'S KEEPER

Geoff

There are two things in every professional athlete's life that are worse than losing.

Being injured and being released.

At the beginning of 2011, neither of these issues seemed like a looming threat. I was projected to be the starting right guard after successfully switching to that position for the last 11 games of 2010. I was feeling so great about my future that I decided to spring a surprise on Meridith. I convinced her to come to a baseball tournament in Myrtle Beach, South Carolina, to see the high school team I'd been working with.

After the tournament, I suggested going to the beach, which Meridith loves. We were lying on our blanket having a great time when I made my move. I dropped to one knee—all those lineman drills finally came in handy for something other than blocking 270-pound headhunters—and I proposed to the gorgeous, sexy, compassionate, whip smart woman who had captured my heart.

I didn't think most women would expect to be proposed to during a baseball-filled weekend, or on a beach blanket. So I totally surprised Meridith.

She said yes.

But while my personal life was riding high, the whole dynamic of the 2011 season felt a little off, a little abnormal from the very beginning of the year. For one thing, all the players spent most of the season training on our own because the NFL Players Association's collective bargaining agreement with the league owners had expired. For another, the entire coaching staff of the Panthers had been overhauled, so I was coming into a team where the coaches didn't know me and I didn't know them.

During the lockout I was working with a trainer who noticed that I was shifting my weight during squat lifts and favoring one side over the other, which meant that I was losing strength on one side. I went to a physical therapist, we did drills and exercises, and I felt as if I was getting better, which was huge for me, because the last thing I wanted was to show up at camp and not be able to perform for new coaches.

The union finally signed the collective bargaining agreement a day before camp was scheduled to begin, which was a relief to everyone involved. On the first day of camp, I was excited to finally start the year. After going 2–14, I really wanted to get out there, work my game, and build toward a winning season. But I rolled out of bed and my back gave out. That had happened before once or twice, so I wasn't too concerned. I got to training camp and I couldn't really get loose. Over the next few days, I had some of the worst practices since I came into the league. My back was bothering me, and my hip was bothering me, too. Instead of impressing the new coaches, I actually got demoted from first string to second string. After all my hard work to become a starter, it was beyond depressing, and it was also alarming. My body wasn't cooperating, despite all my work and focus. Then, about ten days into camp, we were executing a field goal drill and I went to plant my foot for my blocking assignment and my back and hip really gave out.

The next day the team flew me to a specialist in New York who found out that I had a hip impingement—also known as a bone spur—which is when the ball and socket in your hip don't fit together in a smooth, easy alignment. When that starts to happen, you often lose range of motion and suffer tears to the cartilage that lines the socket. For some people, apparently, impingements will go away in a couple of days. So at first, the doctors told me to just wait and rest. After a week of zero improvement, the team flew a specialist to New York who found I had impingements on both hips.

The doctor advised me to have corrective surgery on one

side first to see if that might help the other hip heal, and that's exactly what I did. Unfortunately, that untreated impingement didn't cooperate, so a few months later I had surgery on the other hip.

Recuperating from an injury is never easy, but for me, it's a serious battle. I need to stay active because it turns out I have one of the slowest metabolisms known to mankind. Seriously, it takes a lot of work for me to burn off food. That is one difference between Mitch and me—he can pretty much eat whatever he wants whenever he wants because his body processes food with the efficiency of a Cuisinart. My system takes its own sweet time. As a result, I can gain major tonnage in a few days, so I have to be careful about what and how much I eat. I understand my body very well, now, and how it reacts to different foods, but at this time, my understanding of nutrition and diet wasn't as strong as it should have been.

Still, with all that time healing there were plenty of opportunities to watch the Food Network and to experiment in the kitchen. It was around that time that I started honing the dish that has become a go-to favorite of mine—Shrimp Pasta. One of the reasons I like it so much is that I can play around with it. I can keep it simple, and go with butter, garlic, shallots, and basil. Or I can add extra zing to it with lemon juice or pepper. If I'm feeling decadent, I might work up a cream sauce. Or if I'm feeling ambitious and healthy, I might sauté some light vegetables in there.

I love the improvisational aspect of cooking. Often I'll watch a show and decide to make something similar. It's not like I take notes or anything like that. One day Meridith and I watched someone create crab cakes. The next day we went out, bought the ingredients we could remember, and got busy. As we were mixing the crab cakes up, I couldn't remember if they'd used garlic powder or the real thing and decided to just mince a clove. Then Meridith remembered the TV chef had put dry mustard in the recipe. We didn't have any, but we did have some hoity-toity Dijon mustard and some Gulden's Spicy Brown. Would a teaspoon hurt? I went with the Dijon and fifteen minutes later, we got to find out. Our golden brown crab cakes might have been based on a half-remembered recipe, but it didn't matter—they were fantastic, and the Dijon and garlic added just a ghost of their flavors to the delicious crabmeat.

I spent all of the 2011 season on the injured reserve list, and worked on getting back in shape. The improvement was dramatic; I was pain-free and my range of motion was smooth and wide. I remember not being too worried about my future with the Panthers because I'd had a strong 2010. But it turns out, I was a bit naive.

Actually, I was a lot naive.

Sitting on the injured reserve does not help your cause when there's a new staff in charge with no memory of your previous achievements. The fact is, that staff is invested in playing their own guys—the players they drafted and brought in via free agency. In their eyes, I was the odd man out, a guy who crashed during training camp and might still be a liability. It makes perfect sense that until you can prove yourself on the field to them, you remain an unknown quantity.

When the season ended, the Panthers didn't offer me a contract and I became an unrestricted free agent. I was bummed out and part of me felt a little betrayed—I had busted my butt, but the powers that be on the team had written me off. That is never a good feeling. And I had no idea what my perceived value would be, coming off an injury, so that was a big question mark. Plus, Meridith was still in school in Charlotte, and there was no question I was going to have to relocate.

The good news was that my old Panther offensive coordinator was looking for players for the Minnesota Vikings, and he knew exactly what I was capable of. So Minnesota seemed to offer the best opportunity for me to regain a starting position and I signed a one-year deal with them.

I spent most of the off-season in Minnesota working out and rehabbing my hips Monday through Thursday and then I'd fly home on the weekends to see Meridith. That summer my brother, getting ready for his first year at Cleveland, came to Charlotte and we worked out together, which was so awesome. We would train, watch tape, hang out, and cook.

One morning working out with Mitch, I started to feel something was not right. We were doing sprints, and Mitch was making me look bad. I remember finishing a sprint and telling Mitch, "There is something wrong with me. This is not right. I should be further along. I should be faster than this."

When I checked into preseason camp at Minnesota State University in Mankato, I started getting pains in my hip again. At this point, having been injured and rehabbing for a solid year, I kind of lost it. My mind was filled with worry and dread. Basically, I thought my career was over. I was thinking, "I'm done. I've injured my hip again, and I will never play again."

This kind of thinking is antithetical to my nature. I've always been a guy to accentuate the positive. I've always risen to challenges and fought the odds. But in the blistering summer heat with my body betraying me, doubt about my body creeped in. Even when I went through that miserable draft day, waiting to be picked, I never questioned my ability to play. I believed I could compete in the NFL. Now, for the first time ever, I really wasn't sure.

When I went to visit the doctor, trying to cope with all that panic, I prepped myself for bad news and another year of working on my body. But I also grappled with the what-if scenario that my career might be over. Would I stay in football and coach? Would I go to law school? What would Meridith think?

Of course all this drama in my head turned out to be wasted negative energy because the doctors made a very quick and reassuring diagnosis. They told me I had a sports hernia, which is not a very serious sports injury. It's a quick repair. I went in for surgery in Philadelphia during August and I was back by September.

Unfortunately, the situation I left in Charlotte repeated itself with the Vikings. I couldn't crack the starting lineup because of that damn sports hernia. It's hard to earn a place if you are not in training camp, and I had missed practically the entire camp. So I wound up playing sparingly. I also got the sense that the team had made other guys a priority. Once again, the coaches and the GMs wanted their draft picks to shine. I ended up playing right guard sporadically in 13 games and we finished 10–6, for my first winning season in the NFL, which was nice. There were some other positives, too. I was part of a terrific offensive line that helped Adrian Peterson gain an incredible 2097 rushing yards that season, which was 9 yards short of Eric Dickerson's single-season rushing record. Adrian won the league's MVP award, which was cool. And I played in my first playoff game. Unfortunately, we lost to the Packers.

When I added it all up, I was pretty depressed. I had signed a one-year deal hoping that I would be healthy and play well and essentially earn a long-term deal. But the hernia set me back, and when the year was up, I made it clear to the Vikings that I didn't want to come back. They made it clear to me that the feeling was mutual.

And that wasn't the only breakup looming. My long-distance relationship with Meridith had been awful for both of us. The entire move had been a disaster. I just didn't like it in Minnesota. I was in a small apartment. It got dark for the night at about four o'clock. It snowed. It was cold. I wasn't being a good fiancé, a good friend, a good anything. I shut everybody out, including Meridith, who was studying like crazy. She would go to classes all week, then, every two weeks or so, she'd fly in to Minnesota on a Friday. But we didn't really connect. She was focused on her studies—and had to be ready for tests on Monday mornings—and I was focused on my floundering career and mired in depression. Here we were, supposed to be planning our wedding, and it was impossible for me to focus. Meridith was talking about finding work in Charlotte, which was where her family and friends were. Yet I had no idea where I'd wind up after Minnesota. It was hard to see how we were going to make everything work.

I'm sure if you ask Meridith about this time, she'll say I was totally locked in to my career. And she's right. But I wasn't just self-absorbed for my own sake, I wanted to be able to provide for her and for myself, and make good on the dreams we—or at least I—had spun for the two of us.

I think things really bottomed out when Meridith realized she was having all the wedding meetings by herself and that I was not focused on the details at all. In my defense, I'm not the first guy to want to punt when it comes to the finer points of wedding details. What do I know about placement settings, printing invitations, wedding registrations, and other marital minutia? And so we'd fight all the time. I mean *all* the time. And when I forgot about a previous discussion about the ceremony, she hit the roof.

"You don't even know that we have a string quartet?" she yelled. "Why are we even having this stupid wedding?"

I realized I had no idea what the cake was going to be. I had no idea what the dinner menu was. I wanted to be a part of the planning, at least for the elements of the wedding that I cared about, but I just couldn't.

The fighting and resentment continued and when the season ended we were just so far apart. We decided to break up the first week I got back to Charlotte. I was sitting there, numb, watching a playoff football game, while Meridith moved out of the house so we could have space.

So there I was. No fiancée. No team.

Great.

I remember asking myself, Is this what I really want?

The answer: not really.

When the free agency period started, the phone did not exactly ring off the hook. Not a single team called. I tried to keep calm, but the reality was I was a free agent coming off of two years of not starting and I'd had a total of three surgeries over the last two years. And even though the bone spurs weren't really a "football-related injury," they didn't help my reputation as a durable player. Fortunately, Deryk was out there floating my name, reminding general managers of my success at Carolina, and that I was part of the line that supported Adrian Peterson. Finally, one week in, I got a call from Kansas City.

I flew into Kansas City and the visit went great. I enjoyed

myself there, which was good because, frankly, I didn't have a lot of options. Even if I had hated it, I would have stayed. So I signed another one-year deal.

I was twenty-six years old, and poised to enter the prime of my career, but here I was thrilled to have just latched on to a team. This was not where I wanted to be at all. After confronting and overcoming three injuries, I was concerned about job security and longevity. I wanted to find a stable situation not just for me, but if I ever wanted to have a shot at making a go with Meridith, I needed a secure deal. To do that, I needed to be viewed as a reliable cornerstone of the offensive line, not some fill-in guy who might develop into a starter. I wanted my game to command respect and a guaranteed multi-year deal. To do that, I had to figure out a way to take my game up a notch and make some noise.

The question was how. Luckily, an old friend of mine had the solution.

Mitch

The summer leading up to my first season, I spent a lot of time with Geoff, training in Charlotte. It was great to hang out there in his house, smoking meats in the yard, spending time with him and Meridith, and prowling the baseball diamond again while he coached the Fort Mill high school baseball team in South Carolina. That first part of the off-season was just fantastic.

It was also great to actually work out together and soak up Geoff's knowledge. For the last eight years both of us had played an intense amount of football, but we never really trained together. I had spent most of the last five summers working out in Berkeley, and Geoff had been working at Oregon while I was still in high school.

Every morning we'd go out on the field and toss a football around—yes, linemen like to play catch, too—and do our running drills, stretching, and other stuff. Then in the afternoon, we'd go to the movies, face off in video game battles, or experiment in the kitchen. It was a blast.

That morning when we were out there training, and Geoff turned to me after some sprints and said, "Something is not right," I could see the worry on his face. I was concerned, too, but I don't think I was much help. Other than my own herniated disc, I'd never had a performance-threatening injury that I couldn't play through. And although Geoff had had the same disc problem, and his nasty weight-lifting injury, he had been mostly injury-free, too, until the previous season's hip impingement. I didn't know what to tell him, besides, "You need to talk to a trainer, or the team doctor."

But there was no trainer or doctor to talk to, because Geoff was getting ready to go to Minnesota to play with the Vikings and we were in Charlotte.

Eventually, I had to leave and head back to Cleveland. I'm an analytical guy, and I knew that the immediate prognosis, whatever they found for Geoff, was not good, timing-wise. I didn't need to be a veteran to realize that showing up for camp hurt was not a good way to claim a job. I knew Geoff was aware of this. I could see the concern and worry lurking 24/7 under his California cool. I tried to stay positive for him.

"Dude, even if you get hurt, you will make it back."

"There's no guarantee."

He was 100 percent right. But I didn't want him to dwell on that. "Look, man, how many times have you beaten the odds?"

"Once or twice."

"Geoff, how many players play their first down as a high school junior and wind up playing Division One football as a true freshman?"

"I don't know. Not many, I guess."

"How many guys play through a season with a fractured clavicle?"

"I bet a few."

"BS. I've never heard of one. That killed you, but you did it."

"Okay, so what?"

"How many seventh-round draft picks go from the scout team to starting in one year?"

"That was partly 'cause I was in the right time at the right place."

"Come on, Geoff. Except for your size, the odds have been stacked against you since you started playing. And every time, you've managed to rise above. This is just another time."

I'm sure I was an annoying little brother with a two-year guaranteed contract who hadn't played a single NFL down yet, but everything I said was true. He was an inspiring figure, my brother. He totally helped me get to where I was. I'm the silent, quiet brother. But I needed to be there for him.

"Geoff," I said. "Whatever happens, it's going to be okay. There are three things I know about you: you're a smart, strategic player, you are a monster, and *you do the work*."

Famous last words, right? This conversation and these themes repeated themselves a lot over my first year. Mostly I tried to listen and be sympathetic.

My own NFL debut had been filled with bumps. It's not like the Browns were setting the world on fire.

When the conversation would swing around to me, Geoff, as always, was relentlessly positive about the future. Back in high school, he had predicted that I would be a far better player than he was, even before I'd ever played a down. And he was still sticking to his prediction. It was great getting scouting reports from him as I prepped for games. I loved when he confirmed my own observations. It made me feel like I had the skills to break down tape, like I belonged.

Every player has his own way to watch tape. A guy can watch six hours of tape and really not learn that much, or he can watch for forty-five minutes and be productive and figure out everything he needs to know. At this point in my career,

I feel like I'm a good student when it comes to scouting the opposition.

My primary focus as an offensive tackle is pass protection. So I want to see who I'm going against that week and study his main pass rush moves, because my biggest responsibility is winning one-on-one blocking assignments. Does he try to blow by you or does he juke left and spin right, or is he one of those guys who will try to take you on, mano a mano, and bull-rush in the trenches? What are his countermoves after you shut that first move down? Some of these guys actually come in with rushing game plans, so they might hold off on showing you a move until they are sure there's a passing play coming up, and then they spring it on you.

To help decode tendencies, I also run a tally system as I'm watching film. I watch 3 or 4 games and I can get a good idea of what my opponent's best move is and what his second-best move is. This is really valuable because now I can calculate and anticipate a sequence of events. If I stop one move, I can have a pretty good idea what the countermove will be.

To finish scouting individual players, I study what other guys have done against my opponent that would be good to incorporate into my game plan. I want to learn how to react to certain blocks, front side blocks, left cuts, right cuts, and how my opponent may counter when I get my hands inside.

Once I feel comfortable with that stuff, I start breaking down situational plays. That means I'm looking at how the defense sets up on different downs and different yardage scenarios. What do they like to do on a third down and 2 yards to go, or a third-and-8? Then I also study the team as a whole, I look for blitzing situations, first downs. This is the tactical stuff I love about football, checking through the known knowns, thinking about probability, and trying to turn knowledge into an advantage.

9

RAISING ARIZONA
AND MASTERING THE BODY

Geoff

Leave it to the guy who inspired me in high school to inspire me as a pro.

Duke Manyweather graduated a year ahead of me at
Palisades High. Duke was the only guy on the football team
who went on to play Division II ball. We stayed pretty tight.
In fact, Duke was the first guy to get me into smoking
meats. I went to visit him at Humboldt State, where he was
playing, and he fired up a smoker at his house and started
slow-cooking. I thought it was cool. We had a medley of meat,
and I was sold. Well-smoked meat is up there with some of

the most flavorful foods I've ever eaten due to various dry rubs and mesquite-flavored wood and the long slow-cooking process. After that I started experimenting on my own. Now I'm the proud owner of a Green Egg smoker and I fire it up about eight times a year and cook beef ribs.

But Duke and I had a lot more than a losing record in high school in common. We both loved football, but both of us have taken that passion a step further than most people. We like the science of being a lineman. Although he was never big enough to make it as a pro, Duke used his advanced degree in kinesiology to become a guy devoted to helping athletes move more efficiently. When I got hurt, he was one of the people I called to dissect my injury, what I might have been doing wrong, how I should rehab, what stretches I should focus on, and what muscle groups I should build up.

For more than a year, Duke had been telling me about this revolutionary new way to train. He had hooked up with a new fitness and training company called O-line Performance, masterminded by a former NFL Pro-Bowler named LeCharles Bentley. I didn't know that much about LeCharles, but it turns out that just calling him a Pro-Bowler understates the case. He was honored with that designation for *two different positions*—a real rarity in the NFL. In 2002 and 2003 he was an all-pro guard, and from 2004 to 2005 he dominated at center, his old college position.

After signing a huge deal with Cleveland, his hometown team, disaster struck. LeCharles tore the patellar tendon in his left knee, and his health and career crashed from there, thanks to a nearly lethal staph infection that required two more surgeries. It was so serious that doctors even considered amputating his leg. Tragically, LeCharles never played another down in the NFL, but he became interested—obsessed might be the better word—in optimizing the performance of offensive linemen.

According to Duke, LeCharles was a genius and a revolutionary. He was adamant that the standard NFL methods of training had nothing to do with the needs of a lineman. The old methods, Duke said, built muscle, but not the muscle the average tackle, guard, or center needs.

"You have to train with this guy," Duke would say on every phone call. "Nobody is better than LeCharles. He can change your career."

"I'll think about it," I'd tell Duke.

I admit it: I was skeptical. Not because I didn't trust Duke; I did. But because, when you think about it, who is most invested in offensive linemen? The team and the coaches. So it's safe to assume that it is in the team's best interest to make sure their players are training the smartest way they can, right? And that means all the coaches I had ever worked with over the years must have been teaching similar methods—bench, squat, lift—because they knew that was the state-of-the-art training regime available. In other words, I assumed all the traditional methods were right because, hey, that's what everyone does.

Adding to my ambivalence was the fact that I had trained by myself in recent years and things had generally gone well. I didn't think I needed to pay for specialized training. On top of that, going to work out in Arizona hadn't worked out timing-wise, with scheduling between me and Meridith.

But in 2013, after not cracking the Vikings starting eleven, I knew I had to do something different. I needed to be in the best shape of my life, so there was no way a team could keep me on the bench.

As if reading my mind, Duke called and said, "Hey, I think it's really time for you to explore a new way for you to get your body ready for the season. You have got to get down here and give this a shot."

I remember thinking, "He's probably right. I am not playing well, I'm not as strong as I should be. I don't feel like my body is ready to go to war."

I needed a whole body reboot. And with things cooled off with Meridith, I had no obligation to be in Charlotte. I could go to Arizona and have the time to reshape and refocus.

I told Duke I was ready.

Going down to the O-Line Performance facility in Scottsdale, Arizona, that first time—it's now in Chandler about thirty minutes outside Phoenix—I had some ideas about what to expect. I knew it would be hot—like 100-degree hot. I knew we'd do some strange drills, stuff I'd never done before. And I knew LeCharles would design a program for me.

But I didn't expect to push around two-ton pickup trucks.

I also didn't expect to flip 600-pound monster truck tires.

And I didn't think my diet would change.

But *everything* changed.

The workouts ran between an hour and a half to two hours, and they were brutal. As LeCharles liked to say, "This ain't South Beach. There's no sand, no pretty girls."

The O-Line Performance philosophy is that every workout should be geared to your position, so that the drills echo some aspect of our work on the line. That's why we pushed those huge pickup trucks. Pushing is what we do on the line. So why wouldn't that be a smarter way to build muscle than to do bench presses? The same thing goes for flipping tires. In line-play you often push up against the competition, moving them back. Flipping those tires mimics the hip explosions as we come off the line. And those tires are a lot heavier than a defensive end, let me tell you.

Another part of LeCharles's philosophy is that every drill you perform should be high-intensity during a session. Once you are stretched and ready to go, there are not a lot of warm-ups. If LeCharles thinks you are having an easy time during a drill, that drill is going to get harder. If you are lifting weights and he thinks you are cranking out reps too easily, he'll throw more heavy metal on your bar. He'll increase the friction. Whatever it takes to make you work harder, he finds a way.

Honestly, after that first workout, I felt like my arms could touch the ground—that's how heavy they felt. There were plenty of moments that first week when I thought I might have to quit. But LeCharles doesn't let you quit. Plus, I was working out with some great NFL guys—Redskins' starting guard Shawn Lauvao, Steelers' left tackle Kelvin Beachum, Lions' guard Larry Warford, and the Jets' Willie Colon—I couldn't quit. I needed to represent, and I enjoyed that challenge.

Not only that, but the workouts are so intense that as a player, I developed a new gear conditioning-wise. As my endurance improved, so did my ability to think under grueling conditions. And I look at that as helping me achieve a new physical and mental level—like an ability to shift into overdrive—to give me a competitive edge on the field.

Following his program, I completely reshaped my body, not just by sticking to the relentless workouts, but by eating smarter and better. I guess I already knew some of LeCharles' nutritional tips. I knew carbs and sugar are our enemies, but I thought I could still have a casual relationship with them. LeCharles taught me that eliminating them from my diet would make me feel better, recover faster, and be faster. Nobody had talked to me with the same amount of passion and knowledge. I heard what he was saying about carbohydrates, and how they can sap my energy. I followed his instructions and went cold turkey. I stopped gorging on my beloved fried rice. I cut out pasta. It was hard at first, because I didn't realize how many carbs I ate, how much they filled me up, and how good they are: rice, pasta, bread, fruit. But then I started focusing on eating foods that would help aid my recovery time, like smoked meats that were high in protein and fat.

It didn't take very long before I could feel the difference. Duke was right. I'm forever grateful. LeCharles Bentley became a guru of sorts to me, and I guess I became a true believer.

And, hey, I'm not the only true believer in the league who feels this way about LeCharles and his program. One of the guys I work out with Shawn Lauvao says he'll do pretty much anything LeCharles says at this point. Shawn's attitude is: "If he told me to run through a wall because it would make me a better player, I'd say, 'Okay, which wall?'"

I finished that first March session feeling better than ever, and I immediately signed up for the July camp. In between sessions I stuck hard to my new diet. I remember thinking my body was being reshaped. My musculature felt different, looked different. I felt different. I headed to the Chiefs' training camp feeling—knowing, really—that I had optimized my body to reach a new level of play. I felt like I had made the best investment in my career, and I'm guessing most guys who come to work with LeCharles feel that way. I know I felt like a total world-beater. I was stoked and ready to become a starter again. The big question in my mind was whether the Chiefs would give me an opportunity to shine.

While I was down in Arizona, a blog at *Sports Illustrated* asked me to contribute ten random facts about being a Jewish athlete. I wrote about a bunch of the things I've already mentioned on here, like my kosher status and my passion for latkes. I threw in the fact that neither my agent nor my financial advisor are Jewish. I also mentioned that people are sometimes shocked to discover I don't miss Santa Claus or Christmas trees. As I said in my list: "How can you miss something you never had?"

Since the whole idea of the list struck me as a little odd, I decided to have a little fun. "There is a lack of Jewish groupies. Where are all the tall Jewish blond women?"

I was kidding, of course. Tall Jewish blondes are something of a rarity. And the idea that there are groupies for offensive linemen is laughable. As a group, offensive linemen generally don't have the typical looks of your average leading man, and we don't have the fan base, either.

Sadly.

Of course there was a blond woman that had made a huge impression on me. And even though I was joking about groupies, Meridith was still very much on my mind.

I went back to Kansas City for off-season training and quickly realized that even if the Chiefs didn't make me a starter there was another upside to being in Kansas City, at least from a culinary perspective. The barbecue there was out of this world.

When people ask me about North Carolina barbecue, I have to confess that I'm not a huge fan. That's because Carolina barbecue, or at least the eastern style you get around Charlotte, is vinegar-based. I'm not a huge fan of vinegary barbecue. I don't like the sharp, acidic flavor. I prefer sweeter, tomato-based barbecue sauces, and the Kansas City sauce hits the spot for me. There's a small chain there that is just world-class—Fiorella's Jack Stack Barbecue. I would go there twice a week and load up on barbecue beef ribs, which are flavored with a dry rub and dowsed in the restaurant's signature tomato-and-ketchup-based sauce. I was blown away every time I ate there. And I'm not the only one; I recently discovered that Zagat named it America's top barbecue restaurant. I know there's a lot of Texas barbecue out there that I've yet to try, but so far Jack Stack gets my vote as the best I've ever had.

It is always a plus when you come to a new team and you are in shape. It's even better when you show up in the best shape of your life. From my perspective, I had the best camp of my career. I didn't quite crack the starting lineup, but I felt like I had shown my coaches, the two Andys—Coach Reid and our offensive line coach Andy Heck—what I could do, and they liked what they saw.

My hunch turned out to be right. The season opened and even though I wasn't slated to start, our right guard Jon Asamoah got hurt, so I was his replacement. Two weeks later, our left guard Jeff Allen got hurt in the second half, so I finished that game and started week 4 at left guard. Then, after the middle of the season, our right guard Jon got hurt again. The coach put me in and the stars, as they say, aligned.

In football there are a number of axioms that are 100 percent true. Here are three: One man's injury is another man's opportunity; timing is everything; and never underestimate luck. But you make your own luck by being ready for your opportunity. And this was exactly the case for me. When I got my chance, I was still in great shape and I played my heart out and took care of business on the field. It was perfect timing. Just as important, our team was winning the games I was in, which was lucky for me. So the coaches just left me in there, and that inspired me to work and prepare even harder. I had done so much work to get back to being a starter—almost three years had passed since my success with Carolina—there was no way I was going to let it go.

We finished the season 11–5 and I got to start my first playoff game against the Indianapolis Colts. And what a game it was. We put the wild in wild card with a playoff game of historic proportions—just a crazy, explosive, high-scoring game. About as close as you can get to collegiate shootout, now that I think about it. I mean, really, how often do you see a game end 45-44 in the NFL? Or one where the teams combine to gain *1,049 total yards*? That number is a postseason record, by the way; we gained 513, and Indianapolis went for 536. (Actually, that once-in-a-lifetime experience has happened twice now; I played in the Giants epic 2015 shootout against New Orleans that ended 52-49, the third-highest scoring game in NFL history. The offenses combined for 1,030 total yards.)

It was just an exhausting, exhilarating game. I'm stoked to have been part of that. But being on the losing side and setting a record nobody wants—eight consecutive playoff losses in a row for the Chiefs—was an ending I wish I could rewrite.

Speaking of endings getting rewritten, Kansas City was also the place where Meridith and I reunited.

After I signed with Kansas City and finished my first session with LeCharles, I felt, as I've said, amazing. I was feeling confident about my body and about the situation with the Chiefs, which was a younger locker room that offered a better opportunity to play than I'd had in Minnesota. Meridith and I had kept in touch. We still loved each other, but it was clear we had work to do, and we couldn't do it if we were far apart.

I called up Meridith and laid it on the line. "I'm moving to Kansas City. If we're going to make this work, we have to be together. You have to move to Kansas City."

I knew I was asking a lot. Meridith was about to finish nursing school. She had been applying for nursing jobs in Charlotte, where her friends and family were. She was excited about having a career. And because I had signed a one-year deal, I was asking her to put that part of her life on hold. All for me, yeah, but also for us.

We had more conversations. I told her how good I felt. How much more confident I was and how I felt like there was at least a chance K.C. might turn into a long-term situation.

I also told her how much I wanted to be with her.

Together we decided to go all in. She flew to Kansas City and we set up house. We discovered that Kansas City has an active wives' club. Tammy Reid, the wife of head coach Andy Reid, is fantastic at creating a sense of community. She invites the significant others of the Chiefs' players to her house, organizes volunteer opportunities, and everybody gets to know one another. She creates a community.

And even though Meridith knew full well that we might not even be in town the following season, she made an effort to meet other people and form friendships. I really admired Meridith for putting herself out there because by now the one thing she knew about a life in football is that, unless you are a big star, you are likely to move around a lot, so friendships can be fleeting. Every once in a while, she'd jet back over to Charlotte to touch base with her family and friends, but I guess the whole K.C. thing wasn't feeling too bad because about halfway through the season we were sitting on the couch one night, and Meridith looks at me and says, "Let's get married this spring."

I was a little surprised. But I was blown away, too. I thought about how much we'd been through together: the ups and downs of my career and my health; Meridith's surviving nursing school, which was a rigorous program. We'd been together, we'd been separated. We both knew together was better. I said, "Let's do it!"

We called our wedding planner and got the ball rolling for a California wedding in March. I guess this wedding story isn't really romantic—no surprise rings or elaborate Jumbotron proposals. But in a way, given all our tough times, it felt more romantic than ever. After all the ups and downs, we had endured and grown closer together. I couldn't imagine not being with Meridith.

Then, just when I thought the romantic bliss couldn't get any higher, a second major development surfaced during our stay in Kansas City that drove it off the charts.

Meridith was pregnant, and we were both absolutely— what's the right word here?—thrilled? Overjoyed? Out of our heads?

The honest answer is: all of the above.

And maybe a little terrified, too!

Schwartz Bowl

Geoff

There was one other major event that happened in Kansas City, although incredibly the media failed to pick up on its importance.

What am I talking about? The first ever—and so far only—Schwartz Bowl took place October 27, 2013, at Arrowhead Stadium, in Kansas City.

Okay, obviously it wasn't a major national story, but it was huge to us. Mitch and I never see each other during the season. From August to December, we are tied to our jobs and our teams. So when the Browns came to Kansas City, it marked the second time since before Mitch left for college in 2007—seven years!—that we had seen each other during the season. The only other time was back in 2010, when Mitch's season finished early and he was able to fly out in late December when the Panthers were taking on Arizona.

Naturally I was completely pumped for what was a very special occasion. Our parents were there, and my uncle Fred flew in, too. I'll let Mitch tell you about our dinner, but it was just great having him in town. We both got to the field early and hung out and then I met some of Mitch's pals on the offensive line, which was great since I'd been watching them all for the last three seasons.

When I watch Mitch play, I get nervous. Seriously, I'm more nervous for him than I ever am for myself when I go out to play.

I'm sure it's the same for him. (Right, Mitch? Right?) I just want him to excel. So the Schwartz Bowl posed some potentially awkward problems.

As soon as we found out about the game, we both agreed that we wouldn't discuss any of our respective team's preparations. We're professionals. We're brothers. But our teammates are sort of brothers as well. So game and strategy discussion was off-limits.

Plus, we've both watched enough film in our lives to understand how to prepare. Since I wasn't starting at the time, I was assigned to the scout team during practice. That meant that I was playing my own brother, which is kind of a mind-bender in and of itself. Really, the guy I was going against—our all-pro sack machine Justin Houston—should have thanked me because I probably know Mitch's game better than anyone else in the league. I was the perfect scout.

But it turned out Justin was concerned I'd give away his best moves to my brother.

I said, "Justin, are you kidding me?" It was the tenth game of the year and Houston had been making headlines all season as a defensive monster. All his best pass rush moves were on tape for the entire league to study. I don't know if he was kidding, but I thought it was pretty funny.

Just because you're competitive doesn't mean you're not paranoid.

At any rate, during the week I told everyone—my teammates, my coaches, I probably even told Justin—"I want us to win, no question. But I am not rooting for my brother to get beat." I thought that was honest and showed all my loyalties in the right place.

I only played seven or eight snaps in the Schwartz Bowl, which was the only bummer. But it meant I could watch from the sidelines like a big brother. For every play, I had two goals: I wanted the Chiefs defense to do a great job, and I wanted Mitch to hold his own. That was the optimum outcome from my perspective.

During the entire day, there was one moment that stung a little. There was a play—I'm sure Mitch will mention it in his section—where he didn't fare too well and a couple of guys on the Chiefs defensive squad came over to get high-fives from me. Of course, they would never have done that if

Mitch wasn't my brother. I'm sure they thought it was all in good fun.

I just ignored them. I also thought for a moment about Howie Long's two kids: defensive end Chris and his brother Kyle, who plays offensive tackle. Those guys actually have to face off against each other on the field—something that will never happen with Mitch and me. That's got to be tough on the whole family. I can't imagine what constitutes a good outcome for those guys. Probably just a tie where nobody gets hurt.

Mitch

The Schwartz Bowl wasn't just the first time Geoff and I played on opposite sides of the field. As my brother told reporters at the time, since the Horween brothers always played on the same team, our encounter also marked the first time Jewish brothers had ever played against each other in an NFL game. Somehow I doubt this feat will earn us a place as groundbreaking sports heroes. We're not exactly enduring the obstacles and barriers that Jackie Robinson triumphed over.

But it was a great event for both of us. Our parents flew in, and so did our uncle Fred and our agent Deryk. I think Geoff's pal Duke Manyweather was there, too. The night before the game we went to Geoff's favorite Kansas City restaurant Fiorella's Jack Stack Barbecue, which was just humming. A bunch of my teammates also showed up to the restaurant, including our QB Brandon Weeden. The food was as advertised—delicious ribs. I'm with Geoff when it comes to barbecue sauces. I don't like 'em too sweet, but tomato-based sauces have it all over vinegar-based ones.

And because I'm such a giving individual, I ordered four racks of ribs to bring back to my offensive line buddies at the hotel.

My dad has any number of stories about epic eat-a-thons in which I'm the star. Most of them were when I was much younger and involved going to all-you-can-eat restaurants. And some of them, as you might expect, involve epic bouts of indigestion. I'll spare you the details. This time, even though Geoff ordered us a *ton* of food, I was careful not to overeat. I was going up against a Kansas City team that was undefeated, and the outside linebacker Justin Houston, who was my responsibility, was in the middle of having a tremendous season.

My parents were thrilled about the game. "All Schwartz, all the time," my dad remarked.

"We should have put that on the T-shirts," my mom said.

"The Schwartz Bowl," Geoff said.

"Now that's a *T-shirt*!"

We all cracked up.

"It would help if people actually knew who we were," I deadpanned.

"The fans know!" my dad said.

"You need a Twitter feed," Geoff said to me.

"No, thank you," I said.

"Speaking of T-shirts, we have the perfect outfits for to-morrow," my dad said.

"Are you going to wear all white?" Meridith asked.

"Close. Livie has designed something totally spectacu-lar."

"We don't play favorites." My mom laughed.

"Are you nervous?" Meridith asked me.

"Not really. I think I'll be okay. I guess maybe the TV announcers will be talking about us."

"You should let them know about the Schwartz Bowl."

"I'm sure they will figure it out," I said, glad not to con-tinue a discussion of my nerves. The Chiefs were 7 and 0. I *was* a little nervous. But I also thought I could handle the pressure.

The next day, while we were getting ready for the game, our parents got decked out in their tailor-made T-shirts. In this case, our mom was the tailor, and she might have outdone those "Fat kids livin' a dream" shirts she made for Geoff. She had ordered two shirts from Kansas City and two from Cleveland, cut them in half, and sewed them back together, so that the front and back of each shirt was split down the center. One side was yellow for Kansas City, the other side was brown for Cleveland. The back of each shirt had the name Schwartz, but half the letters were in the colors of the Chiefs, and the other half were in the colors of the

Browns. The Browns side of the shirt had my number on the sleeve, while the other sleeve had Geoff's number.

It was the ultimate Schwartz Bowl item.

Before the game, Uncle Fred and my dad walked around the parking lot to see the tailgating going on. My dad's T-shirt was a magnet for attention. Fans would high-five him when they saw the Kansas City side, and start yelling, "Get out of here!" and booing when they saw the Cleveland side.

But when they finally saw both sides, the tailgaters would say, "Hey, what's going on here? There's got to be a back-story."

My uncle and father would explain the connection and get a swarm of high fives.

Everybody loved the shirts.

I was right about the game and being all right.

Until the fourth quarter.

We were down by six points, with just over ten minutes left, when Justin Houston finally got by me and to the quarterback.

For three quarters I had pretty much neutralized the all-pro linebacker. In fact, up until that point, Houston hadn't made a single tackle or had an assist the entire game. But then, on 1st and 19 (we'd had a penalty on the previous play), Houston busted out on an outside move but then started bull-rushing at me. I met his first two moves, but was leaning the wrong way when the third one came, and he got by me.

A few weeks earlier Geoff had been interviewed on the radio and talked about Houston, who had recorded 7.5 sacks in the first three games of the season. "If you make a mistake, he's going to beat you," Geoff said, "and even if you (don't), he still can beat you."

He was right. I didn't really make a mistake during our battle. True, Houston got by me, eventually, but I tied him up for a reasonable amount of time.

I think fans almost always see sacks as the lineman's fault, and that is often the case. But the rarely spoken truth is that giving up sacks can sometimes be a team effort, too, and sometimes a lot of responsibility rests on the quarterback.

On that particular sack, I think it took just over three seconds for Houston to get to our QB Jason Campbell, who was subbing for Brandon Wheedon. According to some research I've read, most sacks take place within 2.7 and 2.8 seconds of the snap. So—and this is no surprise—the quicker a quarterback passes, the less time there is for a sack to happen. Any quarterback who holds on to the ball for longer than three seconds is putting himself at risk of a sack. Receivers who don't break quickly and make it to daylight on their route are also adding to the risk factor. I'm not putting this sack on Jason—he was out there busting his butt, making split-second decisions as he drops back and goes through his progressions. I'm just trying to put things in perspective. A decision to hold on to the ball for a split second can be the difference between success and failure—that is, my success and failure, and the whole offensive unit's success and failure—on the football field.

If there was any silver lining to that sack in K.C., it's that we wound up pinning the ball on the Chiefs' 2-yard line. As for the overall game, Kansas City came out hot and scored on their first 3 possessions. We fought back, but could never close the gap and lost 23-17.

So I guess I lost the first ever Schwartz Bowl. Not that I'm competitive or anything.

Right after the game, I met up with Geoff at midfield and we ran down to the end zone where our parents, Meridith, and Deryk were waiting for us. My dad says it was one of the most moving moments he and my mother had ever experienced in all the years of watching us: to be down there on the field seeing their two huge football-playing sons wearing different jerseys with smiles on their faces running toward us. And thinking, *These are our sons.*

I'm a grown man, but I'm also still a son. You know what never gets old? Hearing that your parents are proud of your achievements.

Geoff had arranged for a bunch of photographers to be on hand, so we all posed for pictures in various configurations.

Not surprisingly, given the outcome, Geoff's smile might be slightly bigger than mine. But only by a little.

10

THE BRUNCH OF INFAMY

Geoff

"Are you going on a honeymoon?"

It was my agent, Deryk Gilmore, calling me just days before my wedding.

"No, Deryk," I said, well aware that free agency was about to start the Tuesday after our Saturday wedding. "We figure we should stay put."

He breathed a sigh of relief. "Okay," he said. "I think it's going to be wild next week."

"All right," I said, hanging up and trying to stay cool.

It was impossible not to be excited. I had gone through

the free-agency process for three straight off-seasons. But this was the first year I was regarded as a high-value free agent, so I was thrilled to hear those words: "Wild next week."

The craziness wasn't just about football. I'd been looking forward to Saturday, March 8, 2014, my wedding day. I was marrying the love of my life in front of countless friends and family. Meridith had been amazing through these very tough months, and now she and I were ready to tie the knot; the date had been set months and months ago. It was going to be the biggest day of my life.

But now, thanks to new NFL rules, the big day had just got even bigger. March 8 was the day I was going to see if all my years of hard work and dedication to football were going to pay off in a big way.

Under league rules, unrestricted free agents like me can sign as soon at the league year starts officially, which is on March 11 at 4 p.m. Eastern Standard Time. But under the new collective bargaining agreement, there was a seventy-two-hour window of allowed communication between teams and agents before the floodgates opened. For these three days, the agents are quite busy. This is where they earn their money.

The seventy-two-hour window happened to open on March 8 at 9 a.m. on the West Coast—right in the middle of my parents' pre-wedding out-of-town guest brunch.

Talk about perfect timing, huh?

———

If my three consecutive years of free agency had taught me anything, it was that the NFL is a business. I was trying to get value, and teams were trying to get me at a value. Most often, those two positions don't align properly. It's something that's always hard to accept, but nothing that I can't get over. What becomes a drag during the process is the waiting. When I packed up my possessions at the end of the season after a team exit meeting in Kansas City, I knew all too well that it would be a long waiting game until March.

But unlike those years in Charlotte and Minneapolis, when I was injured and not at full strength, this year things were different. I wasn't a second-tier free agent, signing a week after free agency started, I was a player who had fought his way into the starting rotation and stayed there as we made the playoffs. I was holding out hope that the Chiefs felt I was a player they wanted to keep, but I had to wait until at least late February to get an idea.

While agents and teams cross paths at the various college all-star games, they don't talk free-agent business much. First off, it's not legal. And second, it's too early in the process. Teams evaluate themselves first before turning their attention to free agency. But when the rookie combine arrives—that's the time your agent might get the first real indication of the level of interest out there.

Because I was still the property of the Chiefs, Deryk could talk directly and openly with them. He did, and the conversation wasn't pretty. We were not on the same page. Not even close. I got the distinct feeling my time in K.C.

was up. I was disappointed, but I started to mentally prepare to move for the third off-season to a new city. I called my landlord and told her I needed to ship home the remaining items at my place.

As conversations with Deryk continued in the days following, he informed me that the Chiefs still had "interest." That was all. Just interest. I had no idea what that meant. Interest in me starting? Interest in me backing up? It drove me nuts. It was all I could think about for days. That's why I was so excited when Deryk called to let me know that things "will get wild."

He had a gut feeling. I liked it.

I was staying at my parents' house for the few days leading up to my wedding. So when they decided to throw a brunch for out-of-town guests the morning of the big day, I was invited by default. My parents set up a traditional Jewish spread: bagels, lox, smoked white fish, cream cheese, potato salad, and coleslaw, and the required garnishes like tomatoes and onions. For most Jewish American families the bagel has become the centerpiece of brunch, and it sure is at my parents' place. It anchors the entire meal. It defines it. This is both a great and dangerous thing. Great, because these delicious flavored breads—from onion to garlic to salt to egg to pumpernickel—are perfect vessels for a slew of appetizing spreads. Everyone has their favorite combination: white fish on an everything bagel, cream cheese and avocado on a sesame, peanut butter and honey on a cinnamon raisin. But bagels are dangerous—especially to someone like me, with a slow metabolism, because they are silent carb bombs. I suppose there may be denser breads out there—I've had some heavy and tasty German brown breads—but there aren't many.

Guests started arriving, and we were all enjoying break-fast—although I was trying not to nosh *too* much—in the kitchen and the dining room. I knew 9 a.m. was coming up, but in all the commotion during breakfast, I forgot to look at the clock. Luckily my agent was there with two cell phones on him, batteries fully charged.

The first call came in at 9 a.m. and 30 seconds. A repre-sentative from the New York Giants was on the line. Deryk ran into the living room to take the call. Five minutes later, he asked me to join him there. While we were discussing the Giants' phone call, the Rams called. Then other teams rang. This continued for an hour. Eventually, I left Deryk to it and headed back to the party.

Between the wedding just hours away and all the inter-est and intrigue, I wasn't the best conversationalist that morning.

At about 10:15 a.m., Deryk called me back into the living room. It was now me, my brother, my dad, and Uncle Fred sitting in the living room while the party was in full swing. None of the guests had any idea what was going on. They were all discussing the wedding, sharing stories, enjoying the beautiful morning, and the delicious salty synergy of cream cheese and lox on an everything bagel.

Meridith didn't know, either. She was doing what every

bride does on her wedding day, getting her hair and makeup done and preparing for the big event at her hotel.

Deryk suggested we write down all the teams that had shown interest. We decided to rank the teams 1 to 7 based on a list of criteria: money, location, coaching staff, ability to win, state income tax, ease of living, etc. In my mind, it was all about the money, so I disregarded most of the other criteria and sequenced by money. I'd waited so long for this opportunity, and I'd fought so hard to get back into playing shape and dominating the game. My first thought was: let's get the most money possible just to show everyone who doubted me.

Thankfully, my dad interjected, reminding me that I've never made decisions in my life solely based on money. He was right. Earlier Mitch mentioned how my dad was even-keeled as our Little League coach, and here he was, levelheaded as ever. So I rearranged the list. By 11 a.m., my head was spinning. I couldn't focus anymore. I told Deryk we were done with this for now. He headed back to the hotel, and I prepared to get married.

The ceremony was beautiful. It was everything I had imagined it would be. Actually, it was more. Really, it was something out of a movie. The traditional Jewish ceremony was held on a terrace overlooking the Pacific Ocean at Shutters on the Beach, which is the classic hotel in Santa Monica. As the rabbi led us through the ceremony, I remember thinking that Meridith—who always looks beautiful—was stunning, lit up by the gorgeous evening sunset.

Brotherly love. (Courtesy of Olivia Goodkin and Lee Schwartz)

In the beginning . . . (John Solano Photography)

Big shoes to fill!
(Courtesy of Olivia Goodkin
and Lee Schwartz)

First school, then football.
(Courtesy of Olivia Goodkin
and Lee Schwartz)

Beyond the bay! (Courtesy of Olivia Goodkin and Lee Schwartz)

Can you believe we're the same age? Geoff and friends horsing around . . .
(Courtesy of Olivia Goodkin and Lee Schwartz)

Life is but a dream. (Courtesy of Olivia Goodkin and Lee Schwartz)

Always on defense! (Courtesy of Olivia Goodkin and Lee Schwartz)

It's game day, Baby . . . (Courtesy of Olivia Goodkin and Lee Schwartz)

Boys will be boys!
(Courtesy of Olivia Goodkin
and Lee Schwartz)

Love at first sight . . . (Courtesy of Olivia Goodkin and Lee Schwartz)

It's a family affair! (Courtesy of Olivia Goodkin and Lee Schwartz)

Show me the money! (Courtesy of Geoff Schwartz)

And then there were three! (Courtesy of Olivia Goodkin and Lee Schwartz)

Signed, sealed, delivered… (Courtesy of Olivia Goodkin and Lee Schwartz)

I am a Giant! (Courtesy of Olivia Goodkin and Lee Schwartz)

My biggest cheerleaders! (Courtesy of Olivia Goodkin and Lee Schwartz)

My future . . . (Courtesy of Mitch Schwartz)

There's no "I" in team! (Courtesy of Olivia Goodkin and Lee Schwartz)

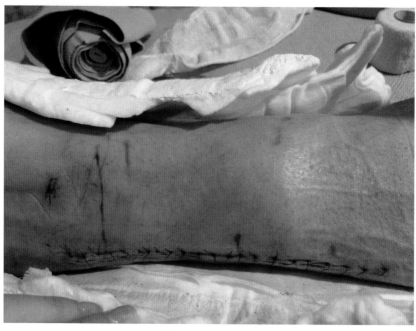

Injured but not out! (Courtesy of Geoff Schwartz)

The ultimate Super Bowl. (David Crane Photography)

Celebrate good times. (Courtesy of Olivia Goodkin and Lee Schwartz)

Wisdom always prevails (Courtesy of Olivia Goodkin and Lee Schwartz)

Touchdown in Love Town… (Courtesy of Mitch Schwartz)

Friends for life . . . (Courtesy of Olivia Goodkin and Lee Schwartz)

Watching film. (Courtesy of Geoff Schwartz)

Family, faith, and football. (Kambria Fischer Photography)

After the wedding, my new bride and I ran off to take photos. Then we headed to cocktail hour. I kept thinking, not only was I married to the most gorgeous blonde with a knockout smile, but if all went well, all my hard work—work Meridith and I had endured together—was about to pay off. What a wedding gift. I went to find Deryk to see where we stood. He winked at me and said, "We are good." We had talked about numbers for weeks, so I knew what "We are good" meant. I breathed a sigh of relief. Now I could truly enjoy the wedding.

And, man, did I ever enjoy it! The wedding dinner was a sit-down, waiter service affair, with everyone decked out in cocktail attire. My brother also gave an amazing toast. He completely roasted me. It was a five-alarm meltdown on my entire life: everything from our dogs, to my Twitter posts, to the cat, to my body. I had *no* idea he had that in him.

Fueled by an open bar, we all did the Hora—the Jewish folk dance where everyone holds hands or locks arms and dances in a circle. The highlight of the Hora at a wedding comes when the bride and groom are lifted up on chairs, and the Hora goes on around them, with everyone clapping and cheering. I had a blast up there in my chair. With all my buddies from the Oregon offensive line hoisting me up and down, I wasn't too worried about falling. Meridith wasn't either, although there is a picture where the casual observer might think she was terrified. Being in the chair in the Hora is a lot like riding a roller coaster: it's a little scary and a lot of fun.

The best part of the night was the last hour. All my parents' pals left, and the crowd on the dance floor was all our closest friends, all dancing. We switched music from Motown to Top 40 and rocked out. People had their shirts off, drinks were flowing. It was crazy. As Meridith and I joked: you know it's a good party when the wedding planners are cutting loose on the dance floor.

It was almost 4 p.m. on March 11, the earliest time a free agent is allowed to sign with a team. Over the last three days, my agent Deryk had been negotiating with teams, filling me in once a day. I didn't need to know all the details of every offer—I was a *newlywed*, after all—just the ones that fit our criteria. By noon, I had two offers on the table, one from the Giants and one from the Rams. We discussed how to proceed, making sure we were on the same page. Around 2:30 p.m. Deryk called and said, "Pack a bag. Be ready to fly somewhere tonight." I packed and headed out to run some errands.

In the middle of errand running I got the call. The Giants had made an offer we thought was great. I needed a minute to think it over. I told him I'd call him back. There was a lot to think about, weighing two teams and two cities against each other. I liked both organizations. New York was the media center of the world, and I've been interested in broadcasting and writing. But St. Louis is a mellow, far less expensive town with none of the quality-of-life problems—aka traffic nightmares and expensive real estate—of the Big

Home-field advantage. (Courtesy of Geoff Schwartz)

Big and Tall. (Courtesy of Olivia Goodkin and Lee Schwartz)

Apple. In the end, I asked myself which team I might regret not going to. The answer, for me, was that the Rams just didn't have the legacy that the New York Giants have—both recent, with two amazing Super Bowl wins, and historical. True, I have no memory of those '50s teams that had Frank Gifford at running back and assistant coaches named Vince Lombardi and Tom Landry, and I never saw Lawrence Taylor in his prime. But just being able to drop those four names—and there are plenty others—that's an incredible legacy right there.

I had a quick chat with my Meridith, and then called Deryk back.

We had a deal.

About three minutes after 4 p.m., the official start of free agency, I was on the phone with the Giants about coordinating a flight to the Big Apple that night. We worked it out; I landed in New York City, and the offensive line coach Pat Flaherty—who has been running the line for the entire time Tom Coughlin has been the Giants' head coach—picked me up. We headed to dinner and had a great time. The Giants' commitment to excellence and to player development, which has helped the team to two Super Bowl victories since 2007, shined through as he talked about the team and the offensive line. I immediately knew I had made the right choice. Early the next morning, March 12, I headed to the hospital for my physical. In the past, I've had two-plus-hour physicals filled with X-rays, MRI exams, and the like. This physical, which was conducted by the same surgeon who fixed my hip impingements back when I was at Carolina, took all of five minutes. When you're healthy, there's not much to discuss. From there, we headed to the facility. I met the staff, took a tour, and grabbed some lunch.

Time to make it official. This was the moment I'd dreamed about ever since I began playing football.

I'd always seen those photos of the players signing their big contracts and had gotten super jealous. I knew if I stuck to the plan, kept my positive attitude, eventually I'd get to this point. So now it was my turn. I made sure to look in the mirror so my hair looked okay. I headed into the assistant GM's office, and there on the table was my contract. I signed it.

There was no photographer, but I didn't care. It was done. All the stress, worry, anxiety . . . it was all gone. I had worked through three surgeries within thirteen months. I had devoted myself to rehab, I had gone to Arizona to sweat and work in the desert sun. I had endured the frustration of all the missed playing time, and all the GMs and coaches passing over me when I knew I could do the job.

Now I could relax. I was a member of the New York Giants, a legendary team with a legendary coach in a great city. I could breathe and look forward to a limitless future.

Then I exhaled, and I thought, "Man, that's kind of funny. Looking forward to an amazing future is exactly what I've been doing in order to get here—I guess I'll just have to keep it up."

TOUCHDOWN

11

GETTING SEASONED

Mitch

My third year through the league was definitely my favorite. It's had the highest highs and the lowest lows. It began with something rare for me: an article during preseason training camp reporting I'd gotten into a skirmish during practice with a guy trying to make the team. The thing was, after we got into it, about half the guys joined in. What can I say? It was hot, and we were into the last days of practice.

Coach Pettine chewed me out a bit, along with the rest of the team. He was right to, I guess. As he says: we're all wearing the same uniform. It's funny, coaches love it when there's intensity during practice, but there's a fine line between intensity and nasty aggression, and sometimes they get crossed and you have to defend yourself. Coaches, understandably, don't like that. And so Coach made us all run sprints after that altercation, a rare punishment.

Looking back on the whole chain of events, we had had a lot of fights throughout camp with zero repercussions. I think since we were getting close to the end of the season coach decided to punish us and set the tone that fighting was done with. And guess what? The message was received.

But maybe the fiery spring camp was a good thing, because the Browns got off to our most successful start in over a decade, going 7 and 4.

My favorite game was against our arch division rivals, the Cincinnati Bengals. It was a Thursday night game in Cincinnati, which is rough, because it's a short week, and you really have to cram all the game planning into a short period of time. But, hey, both teams faced the same challenge. We started the game really well. Our linebacker Craig Robertson snagged an Andy Dalton pass and returned it to the Cincinnati 18-yard line. From there, the line controlled things from our first down with four straight running plays. On the fifth, Ben Tate went up the middle from 4 yards out for a touchdown. Of course, once you establish the ability to ground and pound, passing generally becomes that much easier. We got out to a nice lead and controlled the whole game. It was a really cool feeling. Toward the end of the game, most of the Bengals' fans had filtered out while our fans remained, and they were cheering louder for the out-of-town team. It was huge: national TV and on the road. It was definitely the highlight of my tenure with the Browns, and it catapulted us to 6–4 at the time. Good enough for a first-place tie with the Steelers.

Another highlight of the season took place during one of our home games when two high school buddies of mine, Andy Megee and Grant Lipschultz, flew up from New York to see us play the Houston Texans and against J. J. Watt. It's always great to see Andy and Grant and catch up. I enjoy going out and hearing about their jobs, life in the Big Apple, Andy's fiancé and Grant's girlfriend. This time though, as soon as we met up, they were more amped than usual. The conversation went something like this:

"Dude, you should give us the game ball," said Andy.

"What are you talking about?" I said.

"The seats you got us were next to this girl and her friend."

"We really talked you up," said Grant.

"We got her number," said Andy

"Brooke. Her name is Brooke."

"You need to call her, man."

"We really talked you up."

"Yeah, we showed her your picture and she still said you should call. Incredible, right?"

"Are you guys punking me?" I asked. "How much have you been drinking?"

"We're serious," Grant said. "She's a smoking brunette, man!"

"Totally," Andy seconded.

"We talked to her the whole game. She's perfect for you. I mean, come on! Women who go to Browns games? Who the hell likes the Browns?"

"Oh, just an entire city," I said. "Not to mention me."

"I'm just kidding, man, kidding."

"But she is perfect."

"Yeah, we are not kidding about that."

Eventually I concluded Brooke was not a figment of their imagination. And that they were not, in fact, trying to set me up with a modern-day Quasimodo as some kind of twisted practical joke. I gave her a call. I'm not exactly a rap meister, as you can probably tell, but Andy and Grant said she was friendly and open, and that proved to be very true. I was intrigued at the idea that two unaccompanied babes would go to a Browns game. I know there are a lot of women who are fans, but the crowd at professional football games skews heavily male. We met face-to-face the following week, and I found out she had gone to the game to accompany the girl-friend of one of my teammates at the time. And Andy and Grant were right. She was a gorgeous brunette, with a per-fect smile, and big, mind-melting dark eyes

I consider myself a cautious, thoughtful, analytical guy.

But Brooke pretty much had me at hello. So much so that a year later we were engaged.

———

As you can guess from me being an avid fan of great food, one of the things I like to do with Brooke is explore restaurants. I'm happy to report that Cleveland, despite all the many, many jokes at this great city's expense, has some fantastic food and restaurants. And I haven't even really explored the city's ethnic restaurants. Plus, I've yet to sample unique Cleveland dishes such as the Hanky Pankies, open-faced sandwiches with chopped sausage and ground beef and covered in Velveeta cheese, and sauerkraut balls, which involve fried and baked orbs of 'kraut, sausage, onions, bread crumbs, and egg. But they are on my list.

My favorite restaurant in Cleveland might be Crop Bistro. It is one of the most stunning spaces I've ever encountered. Taking up two floors of what was the elegant United Bank and Trust Building, erected in the 1920s, the huge restaurant, which is built in a former bank and has massive vault doors, reminds me of a small-scale version of New York's Grand Central Station. Interestingly, while the architecture and design feel classic, menu-wise the restaurant has a very fresh take on food. Literally. The chef, Steve Schimoler, uses whatever ingredients are in season, so the menu changes regularly based on what's fresh and what's good. I love that philosophy, and I wish more restaurants had that attitude. I mean, I love novelty foods, but it doesn't make a huge amount of sense to fly strawberries into Cleveland in the middle of February.

My other go-to restaurant is Lola Bistro, which is one of Michael Symon's restaurants. Symon, who is a Food Network star, deserves his fame from where I sit—which is right in his restaurant eating incredibly high-quality, flavor-packed creations. He launched his career with Lolita, and that restaurant is still going strong, too.

The longer I stay in Cleveland, the more I like it. It's definitely different than L.A. Obviously the first thing you have to get over is the weather. Say what you want about L.A., but the climate is close to perfect. I know a lot of people in the Midwest and Northeast sing the praises of the seasons, and I certainly enjoy the colors of the fall and the arrival of spring. But there is something to be said for constant blue skies and perfect temperatures.

I live and train on the outskirts of Cleveland, and one thing I love is that getting from one place to another is a dream compared to L.A. It still blows my mind when it's 6 p.m. and there's no traffic on the freeways. You can find parking wherever you need to. Everything is a little slower paced here, too. There's not the hustle and bustle of L.A., where everyone's trying to get somewhere fast and they needed to be there five minutes ago.

There might not be quite as much to do, activity-wise, but the fact is, outside of the kitchen, I'm not the most adventurous guy in the world. Still, if you want culture, museums, a waterfront, interesting architecture, cool ethnic foods, and music—I've been to the Rock and Roll Hall of Fame and Museum at least four times—it's here for the taking. And the basketball team with that guy LeBron isn't bad. As the opening theme song for *The Drew Carey Show* says, Cleveland rocks!

The next time we played the Bengals was at the end of the year and it was a very different story. After midseason we went into a nasty, inexplicable slide. It was as if all the crisp execution that carried us to a winning record just vanished. The offensive line lost our awesome center, Alex Mack, who went down with a broken leg in the second week of October. Alex was a big loss, no question, but we won some games after he was out, so it's hard to use that as an excuse. At any rate, we were not playing particularly well going into the second Bengals game. The game was Johnny Manziel's first start. I think there's tremendous pressure from all sides when a highly touted quarterback makes his first start. And Johnny was about as high profile as you can get.

So we were riding a losing streak and going in with a rookie quarterback against our biggest rivals, a team that was out for revenge, no less.

They got it.

The Bengals ended up beating us worse than we beat them. I have literally wiped the score from my mind. It was a strange game all the way around. We couldn't get any-thing going offensively, which wasn't Johnny's fault. Their defense was really solid, holding us to 100 total yards or something. And their offense did a good job. They ran all over us. I didn't play particularly well—I think it was one of the few times I've ever had a false start. But this was a total group effort on our part—one of those games where the Bengals were in a perfect groove and we were completely out of sync.

That was 2014 in a nutshell. The Browns were the Jekyll and Hyde of football that year, providing me with the best game and the worst game of my entire career. We started out 6 and 2, and leading our division, and then crashed to end the year at 7 and 9.

Geoff

Football players definitely have a schedule that's unique, and though it can feel like a physical grind at times, I would never complain about it for a number of reasons. First, I love what I do. Second, I think it's a lot better than working a 9-to-5 every day. Now, I say that having never actually had a 9-to-5 job, but I've witnessed how fulfilling they can be. I've watched my mom and dad work far longer hours than that, and I have seen they really enjoy the challenges and the successes that come with office work. I've also seen Meridith go in for training shifts—and nursing shifts in hospitals are often twelve hours or more, which is impressive, considering the life-sustaining work they do—so I know other people have grinding, physically tough schedules. I also know that you don't have to be a coal miner to suffer at work; just standing on your feet working a retail job in the mall or the checkout line at the supermarket can be murder on your legs. Football players, for all our blood, sweat, and tears, are privileged to work in world-class facilities, with catered food, and great teammates all focused on the goal at hand. Third, yes, we work really hard and train almost year-round, but our year has all kinds of different points in it, different seasons, if you will. Here's a breakdown.

During the season players have one day off every week: Tuesday. Mondays we go in from ten until two. Wednesdays and Thursdays, the scheduled hours are usually eight to four. But I like to get in at seven o'clock in the morning, I do a little rehab if I've got an injury, which really means getting hot and cold tub treatments. Then I watch some extra film. Then we work out individually and as a team. Our meetings are over at around four. I usually do one more round in the cold tub or some other rehab-related activity, so I'm not out of there until about five. Then Friday is considered a half day, but I'm still in at about seven in the morning and there are no afternoon meetings, so I'm out of there at about one o'clock.

Meridith and I typically use Friday night as a date night. I think a lot of the guys go out then. Saturday nights, as a night for socializing, don't really exist for NFL players during the season—we are sequestered in a hotel whether our game is at home or away. So if there's one night to socialize or do something special, it's Friday. We usually go out to have a nice dinner, and maybe go to the movies. It's harder to do now that we have Alex in our lives, but we try to make it work. After all we've been through, it's important we have time to focus on each other.

Sundays are all about the game, of course. Home games are a lot easier because there's no travel. It's a fact that football players have it much easier than the rest of the world when it comes to travel—as Mitch says, we don't have to deal with all the lines and hassles that come with commercial flights. I guess only world leaders and billionaires with private jets have it easier than professional athletes. But it's not like we are all lounging in first class drinking champagne—in fact, the only team I've ever been on where players sit in first class is the Giants. Most teams that I played on reserve the front of the plane for coaches. But Coach Coughlin is one of the few who has veterans sit up front and enjoy the extra leg room.

I love traveling and visiting new cities, but travel in the NFL is all about the work you are going to do on the field. Often we arrive in the city that we're playing in around 4 p.m. on Saturday, although when flying from one coast to the other, teams typically fly in on Friday to get acclimated. We get a couple of hours for dinner and to meet up with family or friends in town. We get back to the hotel by 7 p.m. and have meetings and go to sleep. Then we wake up the next morning to play our game and fly home immediately afterward.

Playing a night game on the road is probably the hardest kind of road trip. You don't get back until around 6 a.m. sometimes. And you know how some trips go more smoothly than others? Sports teams have unexpected screwups, too. I think the worst case of adding insult to injury was the Giants in Dallas when we let the Cowboys come back and beat us; that night our plane had mechanical problems and we were left out on the runway for three hours.

Obviously the travel kind of throws your Monday off, but you just deal with it. Speaking of sleep, someone told me that most NBA players take afternoon naps. It's like a lifestyle ritual. They work out in the mornings, have lunch, and then it's siesta time. I guess that makes perfect sense for them, as they play most of their games at night. They probably don't leave the arena until 11 p.m., then they go eat, and decompress, and so I bet their day starts later, too. I wonder if baseball players do the same thing.

For football, though, this sequence—train, game, repeat— is locked in for the entire season, with the exception of the bye week, when we get four days off in a row. Most players use that time to visit family. But it sure goes by quickly, and then you are right back drilling, studying, and planning for the next game.

During the off-season we definitely have it nice. But after the intensity of the season, that can take a little getting used to, strange as that may sound. When we're off completely, it's definitely weird the first couple of days because our lives have been so regimented for six or seven months.

Once the season is over, we have four months of freedom (unless, of course, you make it to the Super Bowl; then you have just under three months off) until the voluntary off-season workouts start, usually around the last two weeks of April. Over the years, Meridith and I have tried to get away on a real vacation at the end of March. Last year we went to Hawaii with eight-month-old Alex. It was great, except for the six-hour time change from the East Coast, which meant that Alex would wake up at 3 a.m. ready to get busy and play. I like to joke that somebody needs to invent a word for "a vacation with a hyperactive baby" because I'm not sure the word "vacation" is accurate.

When we get back from our holiday, I start getting ready for the season and head to Arizona for a few weeks with LeCharles and start my diet again. When I return, the official voluntary off-season work starts. These are nine-week programs, which used to be thirteen-week programs back when I was a rookie. The first two weeks are strength and conditioning and rehab. Basically it is a great deal of weight training. Then there are three weeks of on-field workouts and drills, but those are zero-contact or offense versus defense drills. For those first five weeks, we work four-hour days. I go in at nine o'clock and am home by one. Hard to complain about that, right?

Over the next four weeks we have ten total days of what is called OTA—organized team activity. That's when we have 7 on 7 or 11 on 11 drills. There's not that much live contact, but we do have a bit of hitting. These sessions go on for six hours and I get home at three o'clock.

When we break in the middle of June, I'll go to Arizona

for more conditioning and Meridith will go to Charlotte. Then we meet back in New Jersey about a week before the start of the thing that really matters, the reason we've done all this conditioning: to survive and thrive during preseason training camp.

I think I've talked a bunch about training camp. By now I consider it more a mental grind than a physical one. We are there from seven o'clock in the morning until nine o'clock at night. That is a very long day, and like the combine all those years ago, it's physically and mentally taxing. One of the things I do to help myself get through the day is I take the schedules that are handed out and I cross off the day as it progresses. Of course, sometimes I get wrapped up and forget, but then I go back and cross off everything I've done. It's a little thing, but it gives me a sense of accomplishment, of progress. I've crossed off one of my trials and am that much closer to the end.

The Giants hold training camp at their state-of-the-art facility in East Rutherford, near the MetLife Stadium, and I am completely thankful for that. It makes my life a little more normal. I get the purpose of going away to training camp in a remote location. I like that you bond with your teammates and feel like you are only there for football. But having Alex and being able to see him every day because training camp is twenty minutes from my house has been beyond great. It is just awesome.

The grind of preseason is still tremendously draining. If

there's any turning point in training camp for established players, I'd say it's when you get to that second preseason game and the coaches start game planning more. That's the point when it starts to become less like boot camp and more like the season.

12

THE STREAK: STAYING IN SHAPE AND DECOMPRESSING

Mitch

"What's your secret?"

After the usual questions about my size and my parents' size (they are a bit taller than average and have medium builds), and whether I think Johnny Manziel is going to be as good as he was in college, most people ask me about my streak of consecutive games and how do I do it. I've played every offensive down of every game for the Browns. That's 64 games and counting. Add that to my 51 games in college, and that's a pretty good streak. But when people start to make a big deal out of it, I have to laugh. First of all, I've got a long way to go before I can give Brett Favre a run for his money. I am proud of my record. It is pretty cool. But that guy started *297* games in a row, which is truly astounding when you consider he played the one position that comes with a bull's-eye on its back. Nobody will ever admit to trying to injure another player on the field, but knocking the starting quarterback out of the game is the best way to ruin the opposing team's game plan. So the fact that Favre endured so many sacks and knockdowns without actually missing a start is one of the most remarkable records in football history and maybe all of sports history.

Second of all, my record isn't even very notable *on my own team*. My buddy Joe Thomas has started 112 consecutive games and played on every offensive snap—he was up to 6,923 consecutive offensive plays toward the end of the 2015 season—during that streak. He's played nine straight seasons with no sign of slowing down. So I've got years to go before things get serious.

Third of all, anyone who can put together a long string of games—like Favre or Cal Ripken's incredible 2,632 consecutive baseball appearances—owes a tip of the hat to genetics and luck. I know I do.

Obviously I strive to take care of my body as much as possible, especially at high-stress times, like early in training camp. A big part of that is sleep. I'm sure that sounds funny to some people, as if sleep is the opposite of working out. But making sure I'm getting my rest and have time to recover helps set me up for better training sessions. If I come in worn out and tired, I'm more likely to lose focus, diminish the efficiency of my workout, and possibly do some damage. As far as recovery goes, I also always make sure to ice myself. And doing things in the training room, even just little things like stretching or working with a foam roller, can help. The smallest efforts in maintenance and recovery can make a huge difference.

I think the number-one job of the strength and condition staff is not to make me stronger, but to prevent injury. Prevention comes with strength, because the stronger I get, the better my muscles can protect themselves and recover faster if anything minor happens. Over the years, my training routine—and I think many players share this—has been shaped by a pick-and-choose strategy. I've seen so many guys doing different things over the years, and I'll go study them, or ask what they are doing, and if it seems to make sense, I'll try it out and see how it feels.

Eating properly is also crucial. When I'm in training mode, I'm eating clean and making a lot of meals at home and not bingeing on rich food in restaurants. I love going out to restaurants as much as anybody. Actually, maybe more than anybody! But the menus and all that choice make it tough to eat right sometimes. It's easier to eat right when I'm eating in.

Ultimately, surviving and thriving in the NFL requires discipline, analytical skills, and focus. Geoff and I are guys who have good strength and agility, but we can't be entirely reliant on that. Neither of us has the jaw-dropping raw athleticism that you see with very top picks. There's a clip on YouTube of Jason Pierre-Paul from 2009 engaging in a backflip contest with his University of South Florida teammate linebacker Kion Wilson. The 6'5" Pierre-Paul, who plays with Geoff on the Giants, busts out thirteen backflips in a row to Wilson's six. It is an amazing performance when you consider his 270-pound body and the speed he is moving at are combining to put thousands of pounds—literally tons—of pressure on his hands and arms. He didn't train for that. I mean, I'm sure he has extremely focused workouts and he lifts plenty of weights, but I'm betting he never attended an acrobatics or gymnastics academy to work on his backflips. The guy is just a tremendously gifted athlete. He was born with a body and brain that is wired exceptionally well. That's why he was a first-round pick. Guys with unique elite athletic ability who can maximize their athletic potential are poised to be the best players at their position.

In order to compete against that high level of athleticism, where everyone is strong and fast, and where some guys are practically superhuman, guys like me and Geoff need to make sure we are doing all the other things right. I am dealing with small percentages of how much better I can get here or there. When you put those things together, maybe you are 4 or 5 percent better than the next guy. You're not going to be 50 percent better when you get to this level of competition. It's really about making incremental gains in various areas and hoping all your effort pans out.

———

One interesting—or maybe I should say "tragic"—aspect of the whole iron man thing is that it may be the most marketable aspect of my entire career. It is the fate of the offensive lineman to be anonymous. Actually, despite football's enormous popularity in the United States, football players are, with a few exceptions—quarterbacks, running backs, receivers, and a few defensive players—some of the least marketable players in the sports world. I think that's because, compared to all other sports except fencing and motorcycle racing, football offers the least facial exposure. We all have helmets on during our greatest moments on the field. You can't really see us. Whereas, with LeBron James or Kobe Bryant, or anybody else in the NBA or in professional baseball, you get to see their faces every time they are on camera.

In the football hierarchy, the skill position players are far more marketable. They're the ones who get to touch the ball, and viewers' eyes are on the football all the time. The quarterback touches it every play, the running back gets 20 carries, the receiver makes leaping catches scoring touchdowns—those guys have more recognizable names and they have more recognizable faces. They are the people that the fans want to see. And defensive players are better known, too—they celebrate sacks and ferocious hits as if they have just scored a touchdown.

Offensive linemen? Well, we don't really exist except during replays when an analyst might call viewers' attention to a battle in the trenches. There was an offensive lineman named Jerry Kramer who played for the Green Bay Packers under Vince Lombardi. He wrote a bestselling book in 1968 called *Instant Replay* that recounts an entire season with the Packers. Kramer, who played for at least eleven years, wrote, "Usually, if you play a good game, nobody notices. . . . When you're screwing up and your man is making tackles, you get noticed." Over forty years later, that hasn't changed at all. On the offensive line, you can deliver perfectly on 99 plays in a row and never get mentioned. But if you screw up on the 100th, you can become an instant public enemy.

My dad watches a lot of my games on TV. He told me that during our game against the Texans in 2014, every time J. J. Watt got past me—even if it wasn't a sack—announcers would point out Watt's effort. But the vast majority of the time I stopped Watt and even knocked him down a bunch. Was that work ever discussed? Nope.

While I can really zoom in on the mental aspects of football, the strategy, the film sessions to decode my opponent's tendencies, the biomechanics of our drills, I think it is also important to be able to decompress, relax, and have fun. My other non-football obsession besides cooking and food revolves around video games.

I've been playing video games as long as I can remember. You know how some people can spend hours discussing the TV shows they love, or the music and bands they idolize? I'm that way about gaming, and I'm especially that way when it comes to sports games. I'm a bit of a maniac—

although in the obsessive world of gaming, sometimes it seems like we are a nation of maniacs. One of the interesting things to me about gaming is that, yes, it is addictive, but it is also relaxing. It takes my mind off of whatever I might be worried about—like how I'm going to stop the guy who is bigger, faster, and stronger than me on the other side of the line—and gets me focused on something fun and frivolous. Really, as much as I like talking about gaming— from basic computer games like SimCity and Oregon Trail to PlayStation Halo and Super Mario to Sega's Dreamcast system—I do actually love playing more than yapping about them.

As you know by now, Geoff and I are still both baseball fanatics. Growing up, I loved baseball video games and they are still my favorite type of game. My favorite game of all time is MVP 2005 for PS2.

Tragically for me, the MVP baseball game went out of business, a victim of a video gaming corporate war and the ensuing rush to sign up player video game rights. What happened was that Entertainment Arts, which owned MVP and Madden NFL, got sideswiped when a rival company, 2K Games, made a football game priced at about $20. So a lot of people bought it and EA worried that Madden, their long-time cash cow, was under assault. So EA bought the exclusive video game rights from the players association, making Madden the only company allowed to make a football game with actual NFL players.

In retaliation, 2K bought out the rights to show MLB

players, so MVP was the last baseball game EA Sports ever made with Major League players. It was unfortunate because, in my opinion—and I'm not alone here—the inferior baseball and football video games survived, while the superior ones died.

MVP '05 still lives on as far as I'm concerned. It is still the best game in terms of being able to hit the ball. The bat striking the ball is incredibly realistic. You can tell from the point of contact when you swing whether you've hit a weak grounder or a home run, which is not the case in a lot of games. Similarly, the pitching mechanics are really good. You don't just push a button. I tell people MVP '05 was by far the best rendering at the time, and is still the best today.

That's why every few years I'll start playing the game again. It's out-of-date, of course, missing all of today's young stars, but that doesn't stop me; I'll go back and I'll completely update the rosters myself. It's an involved process. I go into the game, click on minor league players, and then I have to change their names and all their stats in order to update the model for the new players I add.

If you're a fan and a gamer, you'll probably understand. If not, I guess you're within your rights to think I'm a little insane. I prefer another phrase for it: a labor of love.

13

GETTING BETTER (SORT OF) ALL THE TIME

Geoff

The year 2014 was incredible. It truly had the highest highs of my life.

Unfortunately, it also had two of the lowest lows.

But, hey, let's start by accentuating the positive.

As you know, in the first part of the year I had signed the two best contracts of my life—one with Meridith, and one with the Giants. Then I went to Arizona for my own brand of March Madness with LeCharles and the other O-Line Performance addicts. Then I was in North Carolina to see

Meridith. Then I flew up to New Jersey to find us a house. Then zipped back to North Carolina where Meridith was finishing school and entering her last trimester of pregnancy. Then I was back in Jersey for the off-season program and totally excited to be playing for a legendary team with a legendary coach in Tom Coughlin and miracle-inducing quarterback in Eli Manning.

And then, with the perfect timing you expect from an offensive lineman and his super-organized wife, we—okay, Meridith did all the work—had Alex.

Our plan was to induce labor before preseason camp started, so I could be around for a little while. As it happened, doctors told us the first day we were allowed to induce the baby was my birthday. I've never been a big birthday guy, so it was okay to share it with the little guy. We planned to induce on July 11.

The Internet is filled with holistic methods that people claim will help naturally induce childbirth, from going on long walks to eating spicy food to rubbing strange oils into your skin. And we—or really, Meridith—tried a bunch of them. But nothing happened. So at 7 a.m. we induced, and then—not unlike draft day—we waited.

And waited.

The contractions finally started increasing later in the afternoon. And just after 7 p.m. it was show time.

Alex's birth was the most incredible event I've ever witnessed in my life. This unbelievable woman has been carrying a child in her and then there he is. It was just amazing.

n conditioning the muscles around your big toe.
laser-focused LeCharles.

to Charlotte to see Dr. Robert Anderson, an ortho-
geon who is the go-to doctor in the NFL for foot

off the injured reserve on November 17 and told the
I was ready to play, even though I was a little ner-
out my toe. I guess the coaches were ready, too,
our regular tackle was out, so I played the entire
ainst the Cowboys filling in for him. I had had one
in shoulder pads over the last twelve weeks, and
imagine that I was a bit nervous about being rusty.
made it through that game—but part of playing
NFL is playing through injuries, playing through
d playing whatever position your team needs you
So I sucked it up and I did a solid job given my
tances.

e's actually a good chance you saw that game, or at
t of it, because it featured one of the greatest catches
ne: Odell Beckham Jr.'s insane one-handed grab of
d pass in the second quarter. I'm proud to say I was
eld for that. I was looking right at it. We ran a play-
ake with Eli moving to the right. My guy Henry
was pushing toward Eli so I had a good sightline on
When Eli threw the ball, Melton stopped rushing
oved downfield. I was the first guy down there to
ulate him. It was an unbelievable play—not just the
elf, which was amazing, but when you add the fact

We hired a birth photographer and I cry every time I see the video.

As exciting and nerve-wracking as the delivery was, the most terrifying moment might have been our exit from the hospital two days later.

I know everyone takes their baby home and has their struggles with breast feeding or sleeping. It's universal. But that moment when we left the hospital, part of me was like, really? You are going to just let us walk out of here with a baby? Isn't someone supposed to check that we've got a car seat and that I put the damn thing in correctly? But of course they don't. The wonderful hospital staff just smiles and waves good-bye.

Babies. Everybody was one, and almost everybody has 'em. But Alex was a wonder to me. He continues to be a source of joy, love, and discovery every day—even when he has a mind of his own, which he very clearly does.

So 2014 was truly miraculous. The best year ever.

And then I dislocated my big toe.

It was a freak injury. I mean, really, have you ever heard of anybody suffering a dislocated big toe? Shoulders, yes. Toes, no way. It happened during the second quarter of our third preseason game. Preseason games have a number of functions. They let you work on your timing as an individual player and as a unit. They provide players with an opportunity to prove themselves, and they give coaches more performances to evaluate. Other than that, they have no importance to the standings, and they are not even great indicators of how good or bad a team will be during the season. But when the New York Giants play the New York Jets, there's a little more drama in the air. We're the two local teams, and the local news media loves to make a big deal about it.

Getting injured is every player's greatest fear. Getting injured during preseason is high on the list of things you never want to do. And getting hurt in your first big audition for the home crowd, well, that was bitter icing on a poisoned cake.

I was playing left guard, which was a new side for me. I spent my entire career on the right side. I'd played right guard at Carolina, and at Kansas City, but the Giants' line had been hit by a slew of injuries and personnel issues, so I was filling in on the left side. Normally at right guard or right tackle positions, when I anchor my body against a bull-rush, my right leg is back. That's exactly the opposite of my positioning when I play left guard, which requires planting my left foot. I had played right side for so long that my default anchoring was to put my right leg back. I struggled a bit in the early going. Muhammad Wilkerson was really coming hard, and Eli Manning was stripped of the ball by a linebacker (I recovered it) on the second series, but considering the new position, I was doing pretty well. Midway through the second quarter, though, the Jets' defensive end Sheldon Richardson, who is a beast, started bull-rushing me. I momentarily put my left leg back in the correct position, and

then quickly switched legs to get
playing on the right side. And in
jammed my right toe into the
popped out of place. It didn't hu
tried to get off the field on my ov
I couldn't put any weight on it. A
of weight.

They carted me off the field.
Meridith at home with Alex, ar
stands, and how they must be wo
to give them a thumbs-up.

When I got the initial diagno
told me it was the first time he h
years. Unfortunately, there's not
you have a rare injury. Instead, tl
ment swept over me. I was in pai
not being able to play also hurt
contract, and I felt I let the team
by not being able to play, especi
freak injury. I had been totally
and contribute, and now I couldr
pointing feeling.

I guess the injury was also a
in life are out of your control. I
hump in my career where I wou
I thought that with all the work
battles to get fit, I was past thos
and freak injuries are a part of

work
Not

I i
pedi
issue

I g
coach
vous
becau
game
pract
you c
I bare
in the
pain,
to pla
circur

The
least p
of all-
a 43-y
on the
action
Melton
Odell.
and I r
congra
catch i

that he was getting held, and falling down, and near the side-line, he had so many obstacles to overcome and bring the ball in. The thing is, we see Odell make incredible catches like that all the time in practice. He's just a phenomenally talented player who is blessed with huge hands and a great wingspan for a 5'11" receiver. Still, no one who saw it will ever forget that play. What I'd like to forget, though, is that the Cowboys marched 80 yards on us in the final minutes to win the game, 31-28. That was definitely not part of my comeback plan.

Plans are easy to make and hard to execute. That became crystal clear to me the next week in our game against Jacksonville. I went into the game feeling great. A week of practice had me feeling back in the groove. My toe wasn't very sore anymore. I was ready to rumble.

Contributing to my good mood was the fact that we were coming off Thanksgiving, and Meridith and I had hosted a fantastic dinner for the offensive line. We invited all the guys over, plus their wives, girlfriends, and kids. I got to expose my pals to one of my favorite dishes of all-time: the deep-fried turkey.

Like most people in America, I had never heard about fried turkeys, much less tasted one, before I got to North Carolina. But it's a fairly widespread tradition in the South, as I understand it. Obviously, I was skeptical. I mean, I love fried food, but this just seemed silly. One of the glories of a turkey is that slow-cooked, basting-in-its-juices magic, with the stuffing soaking up the fat and brine.

But when I actually tasted a deep-fried turkey, I was blown away.

So blown away that I went out and bought a deep-fryer to make my own fried turkey. It was simple and the results were just unbelievable: crispy on the outside, and moist and juicy on the inside. Perfection.

And it only took about forty-five minutes to cook.

So from then on, I vowed to make one every Thanksgiving. And with my Giants buddies over, we fried one bird and baked another. It was a major feast, even by offensive linemen standards, which are pretty daunting. Between my fried turkey and Meridith's stuffing, fresh rolls, green beans, mac and cheese, and sweet potato casserole, there was a very southern feel to the meal. And of course, at a party with sweet-toothed linemen, everyone brought pies, pies, and more pies. We had about ten pies for twenty-five people, which was about six pies too many, even for linemen.

The turkeys, however, were demolished, as was almost everything else. One thing that is great about eating with the guys is that there's no need to explain the enormous caloric intake. We just eat and enjoy.

I have cooked for my teammates before, but it usually involved distributing latkes at holiday parties. This was just great having everyone over. Linemen spend huge amounts of time together. During the year, we probably spend more time together than we do with our families. Nine guys on the field, in meetings, in the weight room, at the training tables, and on airplanes and buses. We don't actually see each other very much in a non-football context, so it was great to meet the women and kids in their lives. And I can't lie: I loved having my friends meet the loves of my life, Meridith and Alex.

Meanwhile in the "real" world, there were riots in Ferguson, Missouri, over the shooting of an unarmed black man. An Ebola outbreak in West Africa was picking up steam and scaring the hell out of everyone. The news was filled with stories of bombings and airstrikes in faraway places.

I was surrounded by laughter and family and friends. As I remind myself every year, I had so much to be thankful for.

Unfortunately, three days later, in the game against Jacksonville, that aura kind of evaporated for a while.

There were about six minutes left in the first quarter against the Jaguars. We were at midfield and we went into a no-huddle offense. Eli called a draw play for Rashad Jennings. I walled off the defensive end and Rashad got about 2 yards and was hit. The whole pile just fell on me and during the collapse, I felt my ankle give.

Now, I've sprained my ankle too many times to count and I've just played through it. So when it happened, I didn't want to believe I was seriously hurt. I *couldn't* believe it. I mean, I had just finished twelve weeks of recovery from that stupid dislocated toe. This was only the fifth quarter of the season for me after missing a ton of games. So I was lying in the pile, thinking "this isn't terribly painful," and waiting for everyone to get up. But there's a fine line between positive thinking and denial. I was also fighting this sense of dread. You know that train wreck phenomenon, when you want to look at something but you are also afraid to look? That was me under the pile. I wanted to look at my ankle and make sure it wasn't dislocated. Yet I was sort of terrified. I didn't want to be grossed out. Finally, I was able to turn my head and I could see it wasn't dislocated, and I thought, "Phew! Okay! I'm fine." So I got up and walked gingerly back to the huddle.

Then I put my leg down, heard about three crunches, and crumbled to the turf.

The medical staff came out and moved my foot up and down to test the ankle's flexibility. It was fine. Then they checked it, twisting my foot to the inside, and it was fine, too. So I thought, okay, it is a sprain. Then they moved it to the outside and, man, that hurt. You don't want to cry out, if you can help it. That's just not the football way, since everybody plays in pain. But I must have winced pretty bad because that's when the doctor got on the radio and said, "We need a cart out here."

Those crunches I heard? I guess that was the sound of my deltoid ligament rupturing on the inside of my ankle.

Or maybe it was the sound of my fibula breaking, about six inches above my ankle. I'm not really sure.

The break was discovered on follow-up X-rays. When they carted me off, they thought it was just the ankle injury.

Anyway, that's how I remember it. Nasty injuries like that are not the kind of thing you tee up on the video screen and watch in slow-mo. In fact, I plan on never watching that play. Ever.

———

I had surgery on the Wednesday after the game. Doctors attached a plate with seven screws to my fibula and inserted a bunch of pins to stabilize my ankle while my ligament healed. So I have these two zipper-like scars, a six-inch one on the outside of my leg and a three-incher on the inside of my ankle.

The surgery wasn't really the problem for me, and neither was soreness. I've been through enough rehab programs to know that I have the drive and the focus to work my body back into playing shape. That's what I do.

The hardest, most depressing part was feeling totally useless not just on the field, but also at home. Poor Meridith had just finished dealing with me being on crutches all the time with my dislocated toe. And now, thanks to the second freak accident in four months, I had been ordered to keep all weight off my leg for six weeks. I couldn't help out with anything. I mean zip, nada, zero. I couldn't cook, I couldn't carry a clean diaper for Alex, never-mind change a dirty one. I couldn't walk or drive anywhere. I just could lay around with my foot elevated the whole day. It was like I was not even there.

And as frustrating and exhausting as it was for me, Meridith had it far worse. I could make a joke and say that it's lucky I married a nurse, but nurses get to go home. They get to leave the hospital or the doctor's office each day and go to the gym, or meet friends for dinner, or just head home and unwind in front of the TV. With a six-month-old baby and a twenty-eight-year-old temporary invalid, relaxing was not really an option for Meridith. She was a full-time mommy and nurse, or as I like to think of her, a saint.

She took me for better or worse. But worse, through no fault of my own, was winning.

Eventually, the pins came out, the boot came off, and the crutches were relegated to the closet where they belong. I was back among the living, and able to hold Alex and shadow him as he scurried through the house like some kind of ultra-cute crawling machine. And Meridith got some of her life back— she only had to worry about one babe instead of two.

When I went to Arizona in March, I was focused on my ankle and leg—I worked out in the morning with LeCharles and then I went to a sports rehabilitation center in the afternoon to build up the ankle's stability and mobility. Doing things like just standing on one leg can become an important part of a workout. By the end of my two weeks there, I was feeling confident about my conditioning for the 2015 season.

I've got a clean bill of health from the doctors, now, and in the last six months, life has finally started feeling normal for me. After two years of uncertainty and drama and a season of injures, Meridith and I have settled in to a zone of blissful stability, where as new parents the biggest uncertainty in our lives is the length of Alex's afternoon nap. Instead of worrying about my career, I could focus fully on training, and then leave it, and have time for the other things I'm passionate about: Meridith, Alex, my family and friends and, of course, cooking.

14
POSTGAME HIGHLIGHTS

Geoff

Offensive linemen don't play forever. Even my iron man brother may give out one day—although I hope his streak runs a good ten more years. And so I've started thinking more and more about life after sports.

In the last three years I've written a few articles, and those have been really fun. I like sharing my ideas, experiences, and observations about the game. I enjoy my Twitter feed, although that feels more like a conversation than writing. Sometimes I feel that broadcasting is where my future lies. And, yes, it feels great, as a former stutterer, to say with some confidence that I'd like to give it a try. I've been interviewed on the radio and for TV dozens of times now, and I love going on the Jim Rome show. By now I feel comfortable talking and sharing with an audience and interacting with hosts and reporters.

In 2015, though I learned what it's like to be part of a story instead of writing a story—on ESPN of all places. It was pretty funny.

What happened was a writer for Peter King's Monday Morning Quarterback site, which is part of *Sports Illustrated*'s digital empire, called and asked me my thoughts on bringing an NFL team to L.A. I like that Web site. And it's an interesting question. So I gave him an answer that focused on the quality of life challenges for players living in L.A. I said it took me twenty minutes to get to a training facility in New Jersey, and an hour at most to get into Manhattan, but that, depending on where you have to go in L.A., you're looking at an hour-drive minimum.

"The traffic, the taxes and the cost of living are way more than anywhere else," I concluded. "I wouldn't want to play there, and I simply don't think the city needs a team. It's been fine without one."

In other words, the lousy traffic, really high taxes, and super-charged real estate market are not for me. And I don't think it always make a whole lot of economic sense for players with short careers to want to play there. Sure, it's fun. Sure, the weather is great. But there are financial and lifestyle issues.

The guys on ESPN's *First Take*, Skip Bayless and Stephen A. Smith, had a field day with my remarks. It was a real education into how to amp an innocent opinion—of a guy who has nothing to do with actual decision of bringing the NFL to L.A. — and turn it into a controversial story angle. Skip and Stephen brought major attitude and drama to the segment, blasting my opinion for ignoring side-street shortcuts that can cut down drive times, and pointing out that many players would love to play in the entertainment capital of the world, which of course is true.

It was an all-star performance by two pros who, when you think about it, need to deliver controversy, insight, and fresh stories in an entertaining fashion every minute of every hour they are on the air. Getting caught in their artful and entertaining cross fire was an honor and a great learning experience—even if it ticked off my dad a bit. And it hasn't dimmed my interest in broadcasting. In fact, I am actually getting closer to a TV gig than I ever dreamed possible.

For the last few years, Mitch and I have talked about working on a project that involved food. We've kicked around restaurant ideas, gourmet ideas, and, of course, Web ideas.

Then we were introduced to our agent's friend Courtney Parker. She worked in TV production and had heard about our food obsessions, so we started kicking around the idea of a cooking show. It was just friendly chatter, but we liked Courtney's can-do spirit, and the feeling, apparently, was mutual.

"You guys are adorable!" she told us after we had talked awhile. "I can't wait to see two gigantic guys dwarfing everyone in the kitchen, and sharing your passion for food. And, you know, this could be a cooking show that football widows can get their husbands to watch. It will appeal to everyone."

I said, "Courtney, where do we sign?"

A few months later Courtney set up meetings with a bunch of production companies and we did a whirlwind tour, meeting various producers, talking food and football, and exuding the old Schwartz charm—which is really just being true to ourselves.

"This is more tiring than I expected," I told Mitch and Courtney.

"It's like a combine for TV show rookies," Mitch joked.

He was right, but there was a big difference. There was no pressure; we didn't have to perform or pass any tests. Or maybe I should say, the only pressure on us was to be relaxed and ourselves. Courtney was selling us as who we are, two big guys who get totally amped in the kitchen, and who are both passionate about what we eat and how that food can help fuel our careers—or totally slow us down.

The meetings went well, and in the summer of 2015 we shot a sizzle reel, which is essentially a condensed episode. First, we went to a fun and swanky Beverly Hills restaurant/jazz club just off Rodeo Drive called H.O.M.E. (House of Music and Entertainment) and met the executive chef Shawn Davis, who has run the kitchens of some of L.A.'s hottest restaurants. Shawn showed us how he made a couple of dishes, blowing us away with his speed and confidence. Sometimes when I watch TV cooking shows I wonder if everything goes amazingly smoothly because they got two elements that real people don't have—a staff to prep things and the magic of post-production editing. But then, when you see pros do it live, it is an awesome display of fluidity and efficiency.

That is one of the things I love about cooking—there's movement and motion, and all your senses are engaged: taste, touch, smell, sight, and even hearing gets in the act when you consider the message that the sizzle of the frying pan or the burble of boiling pasta sends us. There are not a lot of art forms that use all the senses all the time. I'm sure that sound or taste can impact a painter in some way, but not very directly. Similarly, for playing music, there are many sensory things to inspire a musician, but I doubt Jimmy Page relied on sense of smell to play the guitar solo in "Stairway to Heaven."

But back to our show. After we watched and sampled Chef Davis's food, we headed to a different home—the house we grew up in. And the camera crew filmed me and Mitch working in the kitchen, discussing our plans, engaging in a little trash-talking as I stirred up saffron seafood risotto, and Mitch rolled and stuffed ravioli.

Then we turned to my parents—the couple who raised us as kids to dial back on our competitive fervor, lest we kill somebody while roughhousing, the couple who practically sat on their hands during the Schwartz Bowl because they didn't want to be seen favoring one son over the other—to judge the better dish. My dad, ever the coach, refused to choose sides. So we drafted my mom, and she reluctantly did her duty. I won't say whose dish she picked, because I want you to watch the show, but her decision didn't scar the loser.

Now we are waiting for Courtney to close the deal. I know she was in talks with a number of networks, from the Food Network to the NFL Network. We've got our fingers crossed.

EXTRA POINTS

15

TWO-MINUTE DRILLS—QUICK TAKES ON LIFE IN THE NFL

Geoff on Trash-Talking

Football fans always ask me about trash-talking and the psychological gamesmanship that goes on during the game. It exists, but it's not like the guys are out there delivering nasty trash-talk monologues for an entire quarter or exchanging a constant barrage of "yo' mama" insults. That doesn't really happen.

There's only one exchange that I remember in all my years lining up. I wish I could remember who said it, because it was a fantastic moment. I was playing for Kansas City and we were thumping the other team pretty bad when we lined up for another extra-point conversion. As the snap count approaches, someone on the other team busts out with: "Yo, we have a dental plan in the NFL, go fix your teeth!" I was in my stance and the snap was a second away and I was laughing. It was such a funny dis.

TV coverage mikes up the biggest talkers in the NFL because, hey, that's entertainment. But the fact is guys talk all game. It's not all f-bombs and "screw you" and you're a this or you're a that. You might say things to celebrate a good play or psych yourself up, or you might express your fury or frustration if something goes wrong. A lot of the time it's just, "Great job," or "You got me that time," or "Damn." The exchanges are not always vile or violent. Think about it, you are physically assaulting one another for three hours, you got to say something sometimes.

Of course there are guys who engage in psychic warfare. Guys want to psyche you out. I've talked about how there's a basic parity between players on a physical level, so a lot of what goes into making it in the NFL is your mental makeup. Everyone plays injured; can you play through injuries? Can you play through soreness? Can you play when someone is trying to intimidate you? Can you play well when there are guys talking trash to you? There are guys that have better physical talent that aren't in the league and there are guys—like me—who people might consider not the most physically gifted, and I'm still here rocking and rolling. The margin between me and some of the players who got cut is that I have the mental and emotional focus to cope with the pressure, to keep my cool and perform.

I'm not really into playing verbally charged mind games out there, because I'm trying to stay focused on the game and my responsibilities. I'm not a guy who talks a lot of BS, but even I get fired up on Sundays. I've had teammates tell me they were surprised by my attitude on game day because I'm not like that during the week in practice. You have to have emotion to play on Sundays. As long as you can control and harness that emotion, it definitely adds an edge to your game.

Mitch on Head Games

There's definitely some gamesmanship that goes on between players. Everybody wants an edge. One of the sneakiest things I've encountered is when an older defensive lineman will try to bark out fake cadences to get you to jump offsides. To me, that's a bush league tactic. Everyone is so locked in to moving on the snap and listening for our cues that it just seems wrong to me. We are up there on the line, dealing with the extreme crowd noise and the information getting funneled through the line while running the upcoming play through our head and calculating our opponent's probable moves. It's a lot. We don't need guys adding to the chaos. But then that's the goal of the defense: to create chaos.

As far as trash-talking, maybe the most aggressive behavior I've seen was in our game against Cincinnati. The Bengals were clearly amped and out to avenge their early season loss to us, and so any time they tackled Johnny Manziel or made a play against him, the Bengals' defense would all rub their thumbs and fingers together, mocking Johnny's now-retired "money sign." They were clearly trying to get in his head and upset him.

Obviously, defensive linemen might strut and preen after they do something really good against a team. But it's probably just as much to psych themselves up as it is to trash you.

Geoff on NFL Media Coverage

Every time there's a story on the news about an NFL player failing a drug test or getting arrested it kind of drives me crazy. There's a perception that the league is filled with a bunch of violent, thoughtless criminals, but it's just not true.

Researchers at the University of Texas in Dallas compared the arrest rate from 2000 to 2013 of American men between the ages of twenty and thirty-nine and the arrest rate of the 1,900-odd players in the NFL. And guess what they found?

For most years, the total arrest rate for the general population was between one-and-a-half to two times as high as the total rate for NFL players.

I understand the NFL is a multibillion-dollar business, and that as football players, just by being in the league, we are instantly anointed with the glow of celebrity. Sports teams are these huge, larger-than-life institutions in American popular culture. As players we are part of those institutions.

When a couple of guys in the NFL get into trouble with violence or DUIs or drug possession, I feel those events get because everyone publishes these stories. The media just piles on, obviously because people love to read those stories. It doesn't matter who it is—all-pro star or second-string rookie—it is going to get reported.

If a few engineers at IBM or Yahoo get busted for drugs or a DUI, is that going to make the news? Is anyone going to discuss it on *SportsCenter*? No way! Will there be stories about what's wrong with IBM or Yahoo's recruiting process? Or about how so many employees are out of control in the tech sector? I don't think so.

What bothers me about the amount of coverage is that 99 percent of NFL players are great guys—family guys, great fathers, great husbands, guys who get along great within their communities. Sure, we all have our moments and weaknesses; nobody is perfect. Not the coaches or the owners or the players. But a lot of us give back and work with charities. We do that out of a sense of community, out of a system of values that says that other people and causes are important.

And players are busy, too. They have work commitments and family commitments. The bigger the star, the more special requests he gets.

I like to be able to give back. I like volunteering in the off-season to coach high school kids. I enjoyed speaking at a

Holocaust survivors gala. I'm trying to do more work in the Jewish community, because I've realized how much it means to the community that my brother and I represent another side of Jewish men.

You can bet there are plenty of guys who do a lot more than I do. And yet their actions are overshadowed by a few guys who weren't thinking, who were used to maybe bending rules, who lashed out in anger. Are there players with serious issues in the NFL? Of course. But it makes me mad when these ugly stories dominate the conversation. It is not a true representation of the NFL and the vast majority of the players.

Mitch on Travel in the NFL

People always ask me about traveling in the NFL. What are the private jets like?

I don't know where this idea comes from. It's not like we're zipping around on Learjets outfitted with slick ultra-modern furniture. Although that may be how the owners travel.

We fly commercial planes that are leased from major airlines. Cleveland seems to be a major hub for United, so that is what the Browns fly. Although these are commercial planes, the experience is a lot nicer and more hassle-free than a regularly scheduled commercial flight.

The coolest thing is that we're able to drive our cars to

the airport and park right next to the airplane in the hangar. There's always a TSA security screening next to the plane, so we go through that and just pop right onto the plane.

There are no assigned seats but, at least on the Browns, some of the veterans have staked out standard positions, and you either avoid them or you'll get booted to a different area. If you are lucky, you'll get your own row. But at most two guys will share a row of three seats. We are definitely not cramped together, and we definitely do not go hungry. The air hostesses always have a lot of food options—such as Dove bars and candy—that I rarely see on commercial flights.

The flights are low-key. Most guys listen to music, watch movies, play video games, or read. Or sleep. The same stuff everyone else does on planes.

After the game, there's not a huge amount of time. We shower and maybe have a few minutes to have a postgame chat with any family or friends that were at the game. Then— and this was surprising to me when it first happened—there will usually be a TSA security check right there at the stadium, so we are screened before we get on the bus. When the bus pulls up to the plane at the airport, we all hop in.

Geoff on Prayer in Football

Pregame prayer sessions are a tradition in football. We didn't do that on my high school team, but when I got to college teams had prayer sessions, and the pros have them, too.

Basically all that happens is the coach leads players in the Lord's Prayer. It has never struck me as a big dramatic event—it's just part of the pregame that gives some players comfort, and I think that's totally fine. I don't participate in it, and nobody has ever bothered me about it.

I guess different teams and coaches have different styles. Mitch told me that the Browns have thirty seconds of silence so people can pray—or not pray—however they want to. That makes sense to me, too. Whatever comforts the players.

I couldn't resist telling Mitch that with the luck the Browns have had, a team prayer might not be a bad idea.

For some reason he didn't laugh.

Mitch on O-Line Performance

I did the O-Line Performance experience with Geoff in the spring and summer of 2013. It was a little weird for me, being that LeCharles and the Cleveland Browns have had a rocky history together. But Geoff was raving about it, and I figured I should give it a shot.

It was a great experience. Totally focused and well-thought-out.

LeCharles works different muscle groups that don't always get focused on in the weight room, but even if you are doing workouts with the normal muscle groups he has pretty cool alternatives. The great thing to me is that you end up working out of a position that echoes something you'd do on the line, as opposed to a normal lifting position. So the drills feel more practical and useful when you are doing them.

I have had a lot of great coaches at Cal and Cleveland, but LeCharles is probably the best I've ever worked with at pushing me to my limits. He believes everything should be high intensity. So if I'm doing a lift and he thinks it's too easy he'll throw more weight on there. He never lets you plateau or have an easy or off day. Everything is geared toward pushing the linemen to the best of their capability.

That means the sessions can be brutal. Literally there were days when I had to sit and rest and recover for fifteen minutes before I could even move. And that's after a ninety-minute workout. It's that intense.

I may go back to Arizona in the future. Right now, though, I feel like my fitness routine is where it needs to be, so I'm not currently the disciple my brother is. But I could be.

Geoff on Social Media

Twitter and social media have changed the world in radical ways. It is a great way to share information. I love how fast news of a terrific play—like Odell Beckham Jr.'s catch—can just explode around the world. It's great that people are able to share opinions so easily, but it's also created some negative side effects, like Twitter mobs, trolls, and extensive bad press if you mis-Tweet.

It makes you think twice about going on social media and weighing in on important subjects—or even innocent subjects—because you don't know how people are going to take it. It's just not worth the explaining and clarifying, or enduring trolling. Sometimes I wonder if I'm better off just not sharing my opinion at all.

Mitch on Penalties

I've had a holding call or two I thought were bogus calls by the ref. When that happens, I get pretty upset, but I make sure to shake it off immediately and refocus. Later, I'll go back and look at the film the next day and try to figure out who screwed up: me or the referee. Often, it winds up being a gray-area judgment call.

There are times, though, when it is clear-cut. And, for me, that's the rare instance where I'm holding on purpose. It doesn't happen too often, but if I get beat and I don't want the guy to get my quarterback, I just hold 'em. To me, that's the better alternative to letting my quarterback get sacked. It stinks because I got beat, but holding can be the best alternative for a bad situation.

As for false starts, I think some players might not care about them as much as coaches do. Every yard matters, which is true, of course. And false starts can be frustrating. But even if a lineman commits a false start, it might not be the lineman's fault. A lot of times there's miscommunication at some point. The quarterback will call one cadence in the huddle and then go into a different cadence at the line, and you're locked into your assignment and you don't really hear the change. Or it's incredibly noisy and a change doesn't get echoed down the line and you are the only one who jumps. Or a new quarterback is subbed in and his rhythms are different than the guy you are used to working with. Yes, the lineman jumped. Is it his fault? Not always.

And there's one other reason a lineman may jump off-sides that the announcers in the booth would have no way of knowing. Sometimes, on some teams—never with the Browns and our awesome Alex Mack—a center may miss his cue, and so a guard or tackle might get out of the gate before the ball has moved. In instances like this, the guy who gets flagged is usually raked over the coals, but in that instance, he's sort of blameless.

Geoff on Game-Planning

Game-planning is really one of the most interesting aspects of football. Coaches do the bulk of it on Mondays and Tuesdays during the season, but they game-plan every night, really, breaking down film and devising plays and strategies to exploit what they see, and ultimately creating a situational road map for what we'll be doing on Sunday. Then they map these plays out on paper—there are even computer programs online to track and format things—and position coaches hand the plans out during our meetings. It's our job to learn 'em as quickly as we can. We don't have that much time, but this is one aspect of the game that has always come easily to me. I understand how to play this game from a mental perspective and it's helped me because I'm a guy who coaches can rely on, who's not going to make mental mistakes. I'm able to absorb a game plan and go out and do my job. It makes a big difference, because at the end of the day, all five men on the offensive line have to be on the same page to make things work. The job isn't just about being physically ready. All five men have to know what they are doing, where they should be, who they should block. If you have that down, you end up looking good. If you have just one guy that messes up—from missing a blocking assignment to moving before the snap—it can wreck a game.

One thing I really respect about coaches in the NFL is that, as hard as we work, many of them work harder—although they don't burn quite as many calories as the players. They are breaking down tape at night and identifying the weakest link in the other team's chain, while we are getting our beauty sleep. They are putting together the new plays to focus on. They are diagramming opposition schemes and our responses based on field position, specific downs, and yardage requirements.

In the age of big data, they are able to access an opposing team's tendencies—not to mention our own habits—a lot more quickly and accurately now. But that also gives them more options to consider. The Giants are more focused on data than any team I've ever played on. For better or worse, they grade every player on every play. None of the other coaches I've played for have done that, but Tom Coughlin clearly believes in it. And since he has two Super Bowl rings, I'll defer to his judgment. It's helpful to know how your coaches perceive your execution and to get critical feedback. Hey, if someone is dissatisfied with my performance, I'd like to know about it as soon as possible. And on the other side of the equation, being told I am performing well—the old positive reinforcement trick—feels really good, too.

Mitch on His Teammates

One of the awesome things about being in Cleveland is the offensive line and the continuity and friendship we have. I think offensive lines are often tight, but we have three amazing veterans anchoring the line and they are first-class players and people. It helps when you enjoy the company of the guys on your team, especially during training camp, because you are spending pretty much every second of fourteen-hour days with the same group of people. We're good friends, not just because we work together, but because we get along really well. We go out to dinner frequently. We have potlucks. We cook together.

John Greco, our right guard, may be the ideal Cleveland Brown. He was born and raised in Youngstown, Ohio, where he grew up a Browns fan. He played college ball at Toledo.

I like to joke that he's the team's LeBron James—a local kid who grew up to play for the home team. John is the best chef of all of us, an all-pro cook. His family is of Italian ancestry, so he has completely nailed a lot of Italian cuisine. But he is fantastic at improvising in the kitchen, too. When we were hanging out, people gravitate toward his dishes. A couple of years ago on a Sunday night after a game we got together and were just hanging out watching some football. We put up some pork shoulders on a smoker, and the shoulders cooked for about fourteen hours. The next day he pulled them out and wrapped them up until the late afternoon. Then he whipped up a seafood mac and cheese. Together, it was edible bliss.

I've talked a bunch about Joe Thomas. He is a true outdoorsman, totally into hunting and fishing and eating what he has caught. I mean, when Joe was a senior in college, he turned down a trip to New York to attend the NFL draft in order to go fishing on Lake Michigan with his dad. He is also an avid gardener. I think of him as the ultimate self-sufficient foodie. And by that, I don't mean he can cook a thousand different things; I mean that he hunts, he sows, he reaps, and he eats. Joe always seems to find time to do charity work and has won a slew of honors for much of his community outreach. As I've said, he's a rock solid mentor and player.

My old Cal teammate Alex Mack is a fascinating guy. In my opinion, he is the league's best center—and I guess I'm

en bounced around, he had been working his whole
this opportunity. And then, obviously, Johnny was
and became a threat to his position. It was a classic
n of Brian being the journeyman veteran, and Johnny
he young rookie who was not really sure how to fit
role.

e was kind of introverted the first few months. He
alk to many people.

en Brian was named the starter during training camp,
started to come out of his shell a little bit. I think
oth had a sense of where they were and it wasn't so
rd. I think that was good for both of them to have
learly defined roles. Then Johnny got more comfort-
d started talking and hanging out more.

all started to really like him. He's a cool kid. He's
so he likes to have fun. You'd be hard-pressed to find
on the team that don't enjoy his company.

funny: the Browns have Joe Thomas, who is so good,
ing to be a first-ballot Hall of Famer. But in terms of
otential and fan adoration, Johnny is a whole other
Ve are all water boys compared to that guy. The fans
s for him; they come to watch training camp and he is
in event. I'll be signing a football for a kid and he'll
nny 100 yards away and the kid will start screaming
nny while I'm right in front of him. It's like I cease to
That's pretty magnetic. They love him.

l of course that love is understandable; he was exciting

not alone in that opinion, as he has one of the biggest contracts in the NFL. He may also be one of the smartest guys
in the league, too: he won the Draddy Award as college
football's top scholar athlete. He's a huge travel buff. Every
year it seems like he goes to three or four different places.
My rookie year he went to visit troops in Afghanistan and
Kyrgyzstan.

So you can see I'm not just blowing smoke when I say
my closest teammates are tremendously smart, adventurous, talented guys. It is an honor and pleasure to play with
them. Seriously. I consider myself lucky to work with them.

Geoff on the Giants

People talk about leadership a lot in sports. I really didn't
give leadership much thought as a benchmark when I was
making my decision to come to the Giants. I mean, I knew
Coach Tom Coughlin and Eli Manning had won two Super
Bowl championships together, and that had my attention—I
wanted to be part of a winning culture. But I never asked
myself why they won.

Now that I've been here nearly two years, I can see why.

Coughlin is an incredible coach. Just his energy level
alone can motivate the team. For a guy in his late sixties to
put in eighty to a hundred hours a week, and to be completely focused, well, that is truly leading by example.

Another great thing about him is that he is the polar opposite of some other recent New York coaches. There's no bluster, just honesty and insight.

And when he does aim to inspire, he chooses short, no-BS quotes, which have clear, instructive messages, like, "Be where your feet are," which means stay centered and focused on the task at hand, whether it's lifting weights or exploding off the line to make sure we get a first down on third and one.

I often say football is a lot more mental than people realize, and many of these "Coughlinisms" are offered up as a way to focus players, and to help us control our aggression in the most effective way. Coach gave us one from legendary basketball coach John Wooden, "Be quick, but don't hurry," which to me is about being efficient and preparing yourself in a thorough, focused manner. These adages can help inspire and direct a player throughout the day.

When you take those things together, it feels like a focused, strategically conceived environment. There are times when I feel it is a privilege to learn, to watch, and to be led.

I feel the same way about working with Eli Manning. He is the most impressive guy on the team. He's been the quarterback for twelve years in the biggest media market in the world and he has conducted himself like the consummate pro.

Sometimes he gets beaten up in the tabloids and on talk radio, but he never loses his cool. He never outsources losses, although there is almost always plenty of blame to

share in every loss. He just remains
matic. There are no diva moments wi
guy is extremely competitive, but he's
doesn't affect him, he just comes to w

And really, the man has been mind-
his job. I thought it was ironic at the
season, when we had some tough loss
ment was questioned. This is a guy wl
greatest late-game and late-season con
of the game.

Maybe he has some sort of secret s
don't know about—shrinks, gurus, w
in those golden Manning genes. But
pressure he faces, however he does it,

Mitch on Johnny

Johnny's public persona is a little diff
in the locker room. As far as his whol
tion, well, I'm sure when he wants to
pretty hard at that. In fact, there w
definitely tell Johnny was messed u
terms of interacting with his teamm
guy.

When he first got here it was a lit
and Brian Hoyer, because Brian obvi
starter—as a guy who backed up Tor

to watch in college with his shifty running style and ability to extend the plays, so it makes sense the fans are excited. But as a teammate, you need to support the players who are out there. That's why it's kind of strange to see fans have so much positive energy for the backup that they sometimes boo the starter.

I have a lot of respect for Brian and Coach Pettine for coping with the situation, and for our 2015 starting QB, Josh McCown, who also had to endure a lot of media and fan scrutiny. And Johnny, deserves credit, too. He sure didn't try to use his popularity to force anyone's hand.

As far as the drama of Johnny starting and what he brings to the game, I think the coaches were concerned with his discipline on the field. They want quarterbacks to stay within the framework of the play that's called, at least as much as possible. If a play has three receivers in the progression, the QB has got to read each of them in sequence. If none of those guys are open then you can take off.

But it's not okay to just take a peek at the first option and then run and try to make something happen. The coaches wanted to make sure Johnny let it happen organically.

And at beginning of his second season, he was making progress. You could tell Johnny really made it a priority to focus on football. He took better notes, asked more questions, and seemed more at ease around the building. He was also better in the huddle at calling plays and running them. He also seemed more in control of his personal life. There were some days during the season in his rookie year where I could tell he had partied pretty hard the night before, but I don't really recall anything like that during year two. He seemed to have cleaned up his act.

Towards the end of the year and after the season there were some reported incidents with his girlfriend that sounded very scary, like he had really lost control. Football is a harsh, physical sport at times, but violence towards women—or anybody, really—is not okay. Alcohol seems to have been involved in many of Johnny's publicized problems, but that is no excuse. I sincerely hope Johnny can come to grips with his demons, because he is a talented athlete and a fun and engaging person.

Geoff on JPP

When I heard reports that Jason Pierre-Paul had severely damaged his hand in a 2015 Fourth of July fireworks accident, my heart sank. This was horrible news you never want to hear about anyone, never mind you star teammate. I don't know the particulars regarding the accident, but I do remember thinking: damn, some things are just not worth the risk—at least not in the middle of your career.

Yeah, I know, it's easy to have 20-20 vision in hindsight. But fireworks, like motorcycles and really fast sports cars, are on my list of temptations to avoid.

I hadn't really worked with JPP very much, but I have admired and studied his game from afar, so I know he is a Pro Bowl–level player. He is a franchise star who can use his size, speed, and strength in ways that can be impossible to stop.

So on a competitive level, I was really disappointed my teammate—one of the best pass rushers in the league—wasn't on the roster.

It was also just a frightening story about how fleeting life in the NFL can be.

I mean, one minute he's gearing up to sign a huge contract. The next minute, two of his fingers are mangled and he has no idea how he will function on the field or he has just blown a multimillion dollar payday.

So I'm thrilled that he made it back to the team and got his contract status resolved. And I'm also glad he'll continue to line up against the left side of the line during our scrimmages—away from me!

Mitch on Head Injuries

Of course I wonder about the cumulative effect of all the banging and hits on my body and my brain. I think every player does. It is an occupational risk. We all think about it, and we'll discuss it when a story surfaces in the media, but we don't really sit in a circle and share our anxieties. We know it's a risk, but we also appreciate that the league is doing a much better job watching out for concussions and having guys pass their tests before they can go back out. But I can't say I'm that worried about it, and I don't think that many linemen are.

The reason for that is linemen don't have that many high-impact collisions. We battle at close quarters, so we don't suffer like wide receivers or running backs who get creamed by head-hunting safeties. Or like a quarterback who gets his bell rung by a blitzing 250-pound linebacker.

Also, if you have really good footwork ability and really good hand placement, you don't need to throw your head into the mix. I try to use the rest of my body to do the work. Proper leverage and angles are a lot more effective than just launching myself at a guy headfirst. And even if we do crack helmets, since we are facing off in hand-to-hand combat, we generally have a split second to brace ourselves.

To me the biggest threat of head trauma is probably getting kicked in the head when we are on the ground, or if we get mangled at the bottom of a pile.

On a personal level—long before head trauma became such a big issue—I have never been into butting heads with my teammates in celebration. I totally support my teammates getting themselves psyched up before a game and storing up aggression, but some guys get so amped, they really knock heads. I'm not into that at all, and I let guys know. Or if I see a guy on a skull-knocking rampage, when he gets to me, I'll just grab his head with my two hands and lightly tap it. I'll high-five you, I'll cheer, I'll slap you on the back. But helmet knocking? If I have to get head-butted, I'd rather it happen in a game.

Honestly, if the league is looking for ways to protect players, that should be on the list of things to restrict. Can you imagine a playful knock from a guy like Marshawn Lynch? Even if it's a love tap, it's a knock to your head. And some guys run into a huddle and tap heads with nine other guys in a row.

Dudes, I am glad you are pumped up to play, but that can't be good for you.

Geoff on the Changing Game

Maybe it's part of a general culture shift driven by technological improvements, but whatever the reason, the NFL is getting smarter. The way we train is different, and the goals for our training are different.

And by different, I mean smarter.

For instance, when I first came to the NFL, teams were insistent on players being the certain weight. It's like there was a magic chart that someone had devised that said if you play X position and are Y tall, then you need to weigh Z.

Of course that is ridiculous. Players who are exactly the same height and weight don't all play alike. So what's the point of that?

There's more technology and more data that is easier to obtain. Now it's much more about body fat, body composure, how you play, how you look, how you recover. The precise weight, for most teams, isn't that important, and it shouldn't be.

I also think that new, innovative position-specific training methods like the ones LeCharles uses at O-Line Performance are going to gain traction with some trainers. There's still a lot of old-school methodology—at least for linemen—but I've had trainers ask me about things I've been doing with LeCharles. In the often conservative world of football, where it is not always easy to challenge accepted wisdom, this is a good sign. So I think teams are heading in a better, smarter direction when it comes to training and evaluating players.

16

DINNER WITH THE SCHWARTZES

Geoff

As it happens, the Jewish New Year often coincides with the start of the football season. This is sort of a mixed blessing for me. The start of the football season is the whole focus of my work life. It is, as you probably can tell by now, a great passion of mine.

Growing up, however, the High Holy days of Rosh Hashanah (the Jewish New Year) and Yom Kippur (the Day of Atonement) were also major touchstones. My parents stayed home. There was no school for Mitch and me. We went to synagogue and heard the blowing of the shofar, the ram's horn that the Torah instructs Jews to sound on these holy days. On Yom Kippur, we would fast and reflect on our lives and what we might have done wrong and how we might do better.

So I always feel between a rock and a hard place when the holidays conflict with the games. But, as I've said earlier, my obligation to my career and family come first at this point in time.

Fortunately, the two years I've been with the Giants, I've been lucky to have my parents fly in, a journey they make for four reasons:

1. They want to see Alex.
2. They want to be with family for the holiday.
3. They want to see me play.
4. They really, really want to see Alex.

On Yom Kippur in 2015, I went to services at temple nearby with my mom and dad. I was thrilled that they were visiting. Seeing them is always reassuring and a vote of confidence. It was great having the support of the people who nurtured me and supported me. What a lucky thing to have in this world: a loving and supportive family.

Fasting is never easy, but I've become a much more disciplined eater thanks to LeCharles, and so my fast on this day went well. Over the years I had told Meridith about the traditional break-fast meal: the idea is to have foods that are simple to prepare, so there's little work involved. For many

Jews the break-fast meal is a bagel-driven, brunch-like cele-bration. We've atoned. Now let's eat!

But this year, I didn't really discuss things with her. She just said, "I'll deal with it."

When we got home from temple, the table was filled with the most incredible spread. My non-Jewish wife had gone out and got the most Jewish meal possible. We were stunned.

Smoked salmon, a full trout, whitefish, creamed herring, bagels, cream cheeses, onions, tomatoes, potato salad, cole-slaw, dill pickles.

"This is amazing, Meridith!" I said.

"You've got every dish under the sun." My mom laughed.

"I guess my southern hospitality gene just kicked in while I was at the store. I've known Geoff long enough to figure it out."

"It's perfect," I said.

Toward the end of a fast I usually feel great, like I've achieved something. I feel lighter, not physically, but men-tally. I've endured, and I feel energized and clear. Now, I felt all that and more.

We said the blessing of the bread and then began to load our plates, creating our perfect bagels, laden with cream cheese, assorted fish, and vegetables. I hadn't seen a spread like this since that pre-wedding brunch at my parents' house. That was barely a year and a half ago, and so much had hap-pened in the interim. The wedding, signing a big contract with the Giants, the training, finding a new house, moving, the baby who was growing and changing every day and was now a toddler, learning the Giants' system, plans for a TV show, and even my two infuriating freak injuries. If you asked me to dream up all these events two years ago, I wouldn't have come close. I would have said, um, maybe I'll be on a new team and Meridith and I will be married. End of story.

"Wait," my dad said as he was filling a glass with red wine. He lifted it up, said the blessing of the wine, which translates as "Blessed art Thou, Lord our God, King of the universe, Creator of the fruit of the vine." And then he held his glass out, and gesturing to the table, he said, "To our wonderful son and daughter-in-law—"

"And Mitch," my ever-considerate mother added, "even though he's not here."

"And to Alex, the greatest miracle of all . . . L'chaim."

To life.

Words to live by, for everyone.

POSTGAME DINING

GRANDMA'S HANUKAH LATKES

We make 'em on Hanukah, but they are delicious all year-round. Because most people have smaller appetites than we do, we've scaled down the requirements here. But this should make about 5 servings.

5 potatoes
1 onion
2 eggs
1 cup cooking oil
Matzo meal (or saltines or flour)
Salt
Black Pepper
Applesauce, for serving

Powdered sugar, for serving
Sour cream, for serving
Sautéed onions, for serving

1. Preheat the oven to 200°F. Peel and grate the potatoes (if you want to use a blender or food processor we won't tell). Place the shredded potatoes into a large bowl lined with paper towels. Squeeze out the excess water.
2. Transfer the "dried" potatoes back to the bowl.
3. Grate the onion and wrap in a paper towel. Squeeze out the water in the onion.
4. Add the onion to the potatoes; stir in the eggs, matzo meal, salt, and pepper.
5. Line a baking sheet or plate with paper towels and set aside.
6. In a skillet, heat ¼ cup of oil over medium-high heat. Then add about ½ cup of potato mixture into the skillet for each pancake.
7. Fry the pancake on both sides until golden brown, 4 to 6 minutes. Remove the pancakes from the skillet and place on the prepared baking sheet. Place in the oven while preparing the other pancakes.
8. Serve the pancakes hot with the condiments, applesauce or sugar for those with a sweet tooth, and sour cream and sautéed onions for those who like savory.

LETTUCE WRAP CHICKEN FAJITAS

We love corn-based Mexican wraps, tacos, and chips, but they are addictive carb-bombs. Here's a much lower-carb alternative that brings flavor and crunch.

Yields 3 servings

1 Roma tomato

1 large white onion

1 bunch cilantro

1 serrano pepper

1 garlic clove

Juice from one large lime

Salt

Black pepper

2 medium avocados

1 pound boneless skinless chicken breast

1 packet fajita mix

1 bell pepper of any color

1 tablespoon of vegetable oil

1 package Bibb or butter lettuce cups

Shredded cheese, for serving

Sour cream, for serving

1. To make the salsa: Chop up the tomato (discarding the seeds and pulp), a quarter of the onion, cilantro, lime juice, garlic, and serrano pepper (depending on desired heat). In a medium bowl, mix the salsa ingredients together and season heavily with salt, as tomatoes need more salt than you think, and with black pepper.

2. To make the guacamole: In a medium bowl, mash the avocados together with some of the salsa, the remaining lime juice, and salt heavily, and add black pepper to taste.

3. Cut the chicken, the remaining onion, and the bell pepper into strips. In a large bowl, mix with the fajita seasoning.

4. Add oil to skillet and add the chicken. Cook over medium-high heat until golden brown, about 4-5 minutes. Remove the chicken from the skillet and set aside.

5. Add the onion and bell pepper. Cook for a few minutes until your desired consistency is achieved, shorter for crispier veggies and longer for softer.

6. Flatten the lettuce and place modest amounts of chicken, grilled veggies, salsa, guac, shredded cheese, and sour cream in the center of the lettuce leaf. Roll the lettuce up into a wrap. Remember, overstuffing the wrap will cause the lettuce to tear.

MITCH'S PIZZA DOUGH

This is my go-to pizza dough recipe. I first saw Wolfgang Puck make a pizza on TV when I was fourteen, and have experimented with dough-making ever since. It's made me and a lot of my friends very happy. There's nothing like making your own dough: mixing the ingredients, letting the mixture rise, kneading the dough, and feeling its texture change as you work it, letting it rise again, kneading it some more, and then rolling it out into a beautiful pizza wheel, ready for your choice of toppings. Magic!

Yields 3 large crusts

1 packet of active dry yeast

1 teaspoon honey

1 cup warm water

3 cups all-purpose flour

1 teaspoon kosher salt

1 tablespoon extra-virgin olive oil, plus extra for brushing

1. In a small bowl, dissolve the yeast and honey in ¼ cup of warm water.

2. In a food processor, combine the flour and salt. Add the oil, the yeast mixture, and ¾ cup of warm water. Process until the batter forms a ball.

3. Sprinkle some flour on a clean work surface. Place the ball of dough on the surface then knead the dough by hand for 3 minutes until the dough is smooth and firm. Roll it up, place in a bowl and cover it with a damp towel. Leave it to rise for 2 hours. You'll know it is ready when the dough stretches easily when pulled.

4. Section the dough into 4 equal balls. Work each ball by pulling down the sides, as if you are peeling it from the top, and then tuck the "peeled" dough under the bottom of the ball. Repeat 5 times. On a smooth unfloured surface, roll the ball for about a minute. The dough should be smooth and firm. Cover the ball with a damp towel for 1 more hour.

5. Now you are ready to cook, or you can wrap the dough in plastic and refrigerate for up to two days. Remember: wasted pizza dough is a terrible thing.

COBB SALAD

When it comes to cutting carbs but amping up protein, fat, and veggies, the Cobb Salad is tough to beat. We have two important things to say: First, do not pour sweet salad dressing on your Cobb if you are trying to go low carb; we go with blue cheese or another more savory dressing. Second, if you are going to make this dish, you might as well know who Cobb was. The salad innovator was named Bob Cobb and he was, like us, from L.A., where he co-owned the city's legendary Brown Derby restaurant chain. He allegedly invented the dish while creating a midnight snack to share with Sid Grauman, the owner of the famous Grauman's Chinese Theater.

Yields 4 servings

2 cooked chicken breasts

3 hard-boiled eggs

6 strips cooked bacon, crisp

1 avocado

½ head lettuce, about 4 cups

1 bunch watercress

1 small bunch chicory, about 2½ cups

½ head romaine, about 2½ cups

2 medium tomatoes chopped, with interior seeds and juice removed

½ cup crumbled Roquefort cheese

2 tablespoons chopped chives

1. Cut the chicken, eggs, bacon, and avocado into strips or slices.
2. In a large mixing bowl, combine all the ingredients and toss. Dice the ingredients with a salad chopper.
3. Serve with a savory dressing of your choice.

SHRIMP PASTA

There is something about this combination that is a perfect union for me. I think the core ingredients—shrimp, garlic, butter, white wine, pasta—just mesh into one glorious explosion of taste. The ingredients are kind of like a perfect offensive line— each one doing its part for the meal. Okay, enough with questionable metaphors. Here's the game plan:

Yields 2 servings

2 tablespoons extra virgin olive oil

2.5 tablespoons butter

Salt

2 large garlic cloves, minced

2 shallots, chopped

1 pound large raw shrimp, shelled and deveined

½ cup dry white wine, such as Sauvignon blanc

2 tablespoons finely chopped parsley

Black pepper

1 pound fresh spaghetti or linguine

1. Bring a large pot of salted water to a boil.
2. In a large sauté pan, heat the butter and olive oil over medium-high heat, until the butter is melted. Stir in the garlic and shallots and sauté the garlic for about a minute, until the garlic starts to brown.
3. Add the shrimp and the wine to the sauté pan. Stir, fully coating the shrimp in butter, oil, and wine.
4. Put the fresh pasta into the pot of boiling water.

5. Turn the heat up to high. Bring the sauce to a boil and keep it
   bubbling for 2 to 3 minutes.
6. Stir the shrimp, turning the shrimps over, and continue to cook
   on high heat for 1 more minute.
7. Drain the pasta.
8. Remove the pan from the heat. Sprinkle the shrimp with parsley,
   black pepper, and toss to combine, then plate over pasta.

GEOFF'S PERFECT PRE-WEDDING BAGEL

Because they pack so many carbs, I eat my bagels with discretion and discipline. While some people believe in the "closed" sandwich, this can lead to the contents of the bagel oozing out the sides. So the recipe below is for an open-faced bagel to minimize mess and maximize enjoyment. It was the last thing I ate as a single man, but you don't need to be getting married in order to enjoy it.

Yields 1 serving

1 onion bagel, sliced in half

2 to 4 slices of smoked salmon (aka lox)

¼ cup cream cheese

1 red onion, thinly sliced

1 cucumber, thinly sliced

1. Toast both halves of the onion bagel.
2. Remove the bagel from the toaster or oven. Apply a healthy schmear of cream cheese to each half. Don't overdo it; too much cream cheese will melt and run on a just-toasted bagel.
3. Add a layer of smoked salmon over the cream cheese. This is a strong salty fish, so go easy if this is new terrain. Or, if you are like me, pile on a few slices.
4. Place rings of onion and slices of cucumber over the lox.
5. Dig in.

FLANK STEAK WITH ROSEMARY AND GOAT CHEESE COMPOUND BUTTER, SERVED WITH BACON BRUSSELS SPROUTS

We love goat cheese. We love steak. We really love them together. This recipe should feed two, since flank steak is all meat and no bone

Yields 2 servings

2 ounces goat cheese

4 tablespoons (½ stick) salted butter

1 tablespoon rosemary

½ teaspoon salt

¼ teaspoon pepper

1 pound Brussels sprouts

3 to 4 bacon strips

1 small onion, diced

3 large garlic cloves, coarsely chopped

16 to 20 ounces flank steak

1. To make the compound butter: Bring the goat cheese and butter to room temperature. In a medium mixing bowl, mix the goat cheese, butter, rosemary, salt, and pepper until well combined. Roll the mixture into a log and wrap the log in plastic wrap. Place the log in the refrigerator until the log is hard.

2. To make the Brussels sprouts: Cut the ends off the sprouts. Slice each sprout in half and finely slice the sprouts into slivers, almost like a coleslaw but much thinner. In a skillet, cook the bacon over medium-high heat. Remove the bacon when done and set aside on a paper towel–lined plate to cool. In the skillet used to cook the bacon, add the onion and garlic, season with salt, and cook for 1 to 2 minutes. Add the Brussels sprouts, season with salt and pepper, and cook over medium-high heat for 15 to 20 minutes, until the vegetables are soft. Crumble the cooled bacon and add to the Brussels sprouts and stir until well combined.

3. Remove the compound butter from the refrigerator and set aside to soften. Heat a non-stick skillet over medium-high heat. Cook the steak for 4 to 6 minutes per side for medium-rare. Remove the steak from the skillet and place on a plate or cutting board to rest for 5 minutes. Season the meat with salt and pepper to taste, or season with Montreal steak seasoning for a nice flavor.

4. Top the steak with the goat cheese compound butter, plate, and enjoy.

NO-CARB DESSERT: *CHOCOLATE BROWNIE QUEST BARS À LA CRÈME FOUETTÉE (THAT'S FRENCH FOR WHIPPED CREAM)*

When I'm in training, and sticking to the no-carb diet that LeCharles has created for me—a diet that runs from March to September—dessert is only a theoretical construct for me. The one exception is this recipe, which I've given a fancy faux-French name but is really drop-dead simple. First, an unpaid note about Quest Nutrition protein bars: they have an extremely high amount of fiber. There are plenty of carbs in these bars, but the amount of fiber counter-balances things so that each bar has only about 3 net grams of carbs.

So bake these and eat them with whipped cream, because, believe it or not, whipped cream has no carbs.

Yields 2 servings

3 Quest Nutrition protein bars—or any bar with a high fiber content. (Two bars make a nice-size dessert for a 340-pound guy. So adjust accordingly.)

Whipped cream, from a can or homemade

1. Preheat the oven to 350°F. Place the protein bars in a baking dish and heat 'em up for 15 minutes.
2. Take the bars out of the oven, place on a dessert plate, and slather with whipped cream.

GEOFF'S DEEP-FRIED TURKEY

Everyone stresses about cooking turkey on Thanksgiving Day, but this recipe takes less than 90 minutes to get a bird on the table that is crispy on the outside and moist on the inside.

Makes 1 turkey

Deep fryer

Meat injector

13- to 15-pound turkey

Peanut oil

CREOLE-BUTTER SEASONING

2 tablespoons kosher salt

2 teaspoons garlic powder

2 teaspoons white pepper (black pepper will clog your injector)

2 teaspoons cayenne pepper

$\frac{1}{2}$ teaspoon onion powder

½ pound butter (2 sticks), melted

Dry rub (see page 267)

1. In a large bowl, mix all the Creole-Butter Seasoning ingredients together until well combined.
2. Inject the turkey with Creole-Butter Seasoning into each breast, thigh, leg, and wing.
3. Season the skin with the dry rub.
4. Deep-fry the turkey according to manufacturer's instructions in peanut oil for 45 to 48 minutes. Remove the turkey, let drain, and serve.

GEOFF'S SMOKED RIBS

Smoked ribs are an ideal item for those days when you just want to hang around the house with family and friends. I love creating everything-but-the-kitchen-sink dry rubs beforehand. Then I do the prep work, and then just let time and low heat work their magic. You'll have plenty of time to make some side dishes and chill with your people.

Some days I might add extra dry spices to the rub, other times I'll add barbecue sauce to the mix and throw in some honey. But this recipe gets down to basics: meat, spices, and smoke.

5 pounds beef ribs

Dry rub
½ cup paprika
¼ cup black pepper
¼ cup chili power
¼ cup brown sugar
2 tablespoons white sugar
1 teaspoon garlic powder
1 teaspoon onion powder
¼ cup salt
1 tablespoon celery salt
1 teaspoon rosemary
1 teaspoon dried mustard
1 teaspoon cumin
1 teaspoon cayenne pepper

1. In a medium mixing bowl, mix the dry rub ingredients until well combined.

2. Knead the dry rub onto the ribs and let it sit for about an hour in the fridge.

3. Place mesquite wood in the smoker and preheat to 225°F. Put the meat on and add a pan of water on the grill to add some moisture. Let the ribs smoke for about 4 hours. You can leave 'em on longer if the ribs are particularly meaty.

SLOW COOKER TURKEY MEATBALLS

This is a time-consuming recipe. We recommend it for those days when you are home watching football.

Makes 8 meatballs

1 pound lean ground turkey meat

¾ cup bread crumbs

½ cup grated Parmigiano cheese

1 egg

3 tablespoons milk

1 teaspoon salt

½ teaspoon black pepper

1 medium jar of tomato sauce

10 leaves of basil

1. In a large bowl, mix the turkey, bread crumbs, cheese, egg, and milk together with salt and black pepper until well combined. Form 8 equal-size meatballs.
2. In a skillet, cook the meatballs over medium heat so that the sides are slightly brown and the meatballs are rigid and set, about 1 minute per side.
3. Line the bottom of a slow cooker with a bit of sauce and add the meatballs. Cover the meatballs with a little bit of sauce on each, but not too much. Cook on high for about 3 hours (times vary based on slow cooker size).
4. Take the meatballs out of the slow cooker, place in bowl, and cover to let sit. Pour the sauce into a sauté pan and simmer until the sauce thickens, stirring frequently.

5. Roll the basil leaves and thinly slice the leaves for a chiffonade. Serve the meatballs with sauce ladled over the top of each. Top the meatballs with the basil. These meatballs can be served with pasta, but usually we just eat the meatballs as is.